CONTENTS

Costa Blanca → p. 56

Costa Cálida/Mar Menor p. → 78

Trips & Tours → p. 90

Road atlas → p. 120

MAPS IN THE GUIDEBOOK

(122 A1) Page numbers and coordinates refer to the road atlas
(0) Site/address located off the map
Coordinates are also given for places that are not marked on the road atlas
Street m...
A...
a...
in...

INSIDE BACK COVER:
PULL-OUT MAP →

PULL-OUT MAP 𝄞

(𝄞 A–B 2–3) R... to the
... ap

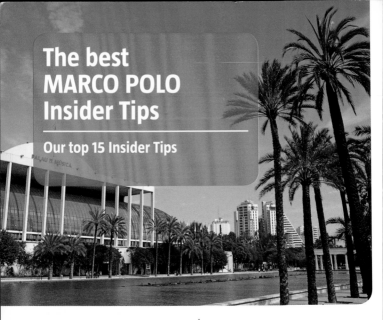

The best MARCO POLO Insider Tips

Our top 15 Insider Tips

INSIDER TIP **Rio-like flair**
When the small town of Águilas pulls out all the stops to celebrate its carnival, the atmosphere is just as exuberant as in Rio de Janeiro → p. 104

INSIDER TIP **Top concerts**
Are you a pop and rock fan, or do you prefer classical music? The Palau de la Música in Valencia has concerts for all tastes on its programme (photo above) → p. 53

INSIDER TIP **Dive deep**
There is a fascinating underwater world of flora and fauna waiting to be discovered off the coast of Cabo de Palos. You will also be able to explore shipwrecks on your dives → p. 98

INSIDER TIP **Castle for night owls**
Life has a different rhythm here – in the summer, the castle in Dénia does not close its gates until after midnight → p. 70

INSIDER TIP **Country flair**
Take a trip from the Costa del Azahar to the mountain and castle village of Vilafamés. It is well worth the effort and can be beautifully rounded off with an overnight stay in one of the country hotels such as El Jardín Vertical, a rustic-style hotel with elements from the 16th century → p. 38

INSIDER TIP **Drop anchor**
It is impossible to imagine Águilas without the Bar de Felipe: it draws tapas fans and is also a social hub – the locals think of the bar as a kind of second living room → p. 81

INSIDER TIP **Charming beach stay**
There are plenty of hotel blocks in Benidorm, but the friendly service offered here ensures that you will not feel like you are just a number: the Hotel El Palmeral is located just behind the Playa de Poniente → p. 64

BEST OF ...

FOR FREE

● **The joys of the saddle**
How about borrowing a *bicycle free of charge?* This is possible in Benicàssim on the Costa del Azahar if you leave a deposit. The roads in the area have cycle lanes, and it is also the starting point for the short 'Green Route' to Oropesa del Mar → p. 43

● **A concentrated dose of art**
The high-quality exhibits in the *Museum of Fine Arts (Museu Belles Arts)* in Castelló de la Plana can be visited at no cost. The main focus is on Spanish artists, and the paintings of traditional scenes reveal a lot about the culture. Ceramics and archaeological finds complement the museum's collection → p. 43

● **Monumental duo**
There are two interesting sights you can visit in Novelda, and you do not have to pay for them: the small castle and the monastery of *Santa María Magdalena* with its elaborate decoration influenced by the Catalan form of Art Nouveau *Modernisme* (photo) → p. 77

● **View of the coast**
Enjoy the free view of the Costa Cálida from the *lookout point (mirador)* in Mazarrón. The small eyrie is located between the Pava and Reya beaches → p. 83

● **Free museums**
Alacant makes it possible for visitors to go to some of its museums free of charge – these include the *Museo de Belenes* with its Christmas cribs and the *Museo de Arte Contemporáneo* with its collection of modern and contemporary art → p. 76

● **Treasures from the sea**
If you want to see all that has ended up on the ocean floor over the centuries, you should visit the *Museo Nacional de Arqueología* in Cartagena; there is no admission fee → p. 88

●●●● Dots in guidebook refer to 'Best of ...' tips

● *Famous rice dish*

The entire region is regarded as the home of the *paella* and the restaurants compete to outdo each other and serve the best. You should always be able to recognise and taste the individual ingredients of a good paella, such as the vegetables, seafood and meat. The *Restaurante Columbus* in the old city in Cartagena is famous for this delicious dish → p. 93

● *Blazing fiesta fun*

Fireworks and bangers are always part of the *Fallas*, a top event in March during Spain's annual fiestas. Artists give free rein to their sarcasm when they build their papier-mâché figures and display them on the streets and squares – especially in Valencia – until the 'Night of Fire'→ p. 53, 104

● *Decorative and tasty*

The orange tree is a common sight in the region (photo). The delicious fruit ripens on countless plantations, and the northern part of the coast, the Costa del Azahar, is even named after the fragrant flowers: 'The Orange Blossom Coast'. You can stock up on fresh oranges at *Frutas Piñana* in Peñíscola → p. 40

● *Total work of art*

The *Old Town in Peñíscola* is a total work of art typical of the cities in the region: a jumble of white houses, cosy restaurants and, at the top of the hill, a castle dating from the days of the Knights Templar → p. 38

● *Commanding castles*

Numerous watchtowers and castles, many dating back to the Moors, can be seen along the coast. In the Middle Ages, the fortresses fell into the hands of the Christians who adapted them for their purposes. One of the most impressive dominates the skyline over Alacant; the *Castillo de Santa Bárbara* → p. 58

● *Beach giants*

The magnificent sandy beaches are among the most valuable assets of the Spanish Mediterranean coast. Benidorm boasts two gigantic stretches of sand: the *Platja de Llevant* and *Platja de Ponent* → p. 63

ONLY IN

BEST OF ...

● *Art and science*

There is no need to be at a loss about what to do if it does happen to rain in Valencia: you can spend an entire day in the *Ciutat de les Arts i les Ciències.* The *Oceanogràfic* (Aquarium), the interactive Science Museum, as well as the *Hemisfèric* with 3-D screenings are also impressive examples of modern architecture → p. 47

● *Alcoholic test*

High-proof place to get away from the rain: Go down into the world of spirits in the *Bodegas Carmelitano* in Benicàssim. The tour of the traditional cellars also includes a tasting session → p. 34

● *Go underground!*

Can you think of a better place to escape from the rain than in a cave? The formations of stalactites and stalagmites in the *Coves de Sant Josep* on the edge of La Vall d'Uixó have to be explored in two ways: one section in a boat, the rest on foot → p. 100

● *Fresh from the market*

You will enjoy lingering inside here if it rains: the halls of the *Mercat Central* in Valencia are full of atmosphere and among the most colourful in all of Spain (photo) → p. 52

● *Temple of the arts*

The *Museu de Belles Arts* in Valencia, located in a former seminary, attracts visitors from all over the world. It is a temple of the arts of the highest quality, with works by Spanish masters including Velázquez, Goya and many others → p. 49

● *Sheltered by the exchange*

If you should actually need to get out of the rain in Valencia, the *Lonja de la Seda*, the old silk exchange, is one of the best places to go. The columned hall is magnificent and is often used as a marketplace by stamp and coin dealers at weekends → p. 48

RAIN

RELAX AND CHILL OUT
Take it easy and spoil yourself

● *Under palms*
The palm oasis in Elx (Spanish: Elche) is a Unesco World Heritage Site and the perfect place to relax. Just look for a peaceful corner in the *Huerto del Cura* and just chill out for a while → **p. 74**

● *As good as new*
The *Spa Las Arenas* in the *Las Arenas Balneario Resort* in Valencia follows in the tradition of historical bathing establishments. You will feel a new lease of life after your treatments → **p. 53**

● *Good vibes in the holy halls*
Lean back in the pews in *El Patriarca Church* in Valencia, close your eyes and listen to the Gregorian chant – contemplative, full of atmosphere! → **p. 50**

● *A well-earned glass ...*
It is easy to unwind over a small glass of home-made vermouth or traditional kola-nut liqueur. You can buy relaxation by the bottle from the producer *Casa del Papa Luna* in Peñíscola → **p. 27**

● *Oasis of relaxation*
Relax in the whirlpools of the *Spa La Manga Club* and admire the view as far as the Mar Menor: perfect luxury! → **p. 87**

● *Ahoy!*
Take your seat and enjoy the panorama of rolling hills, sea vessels and the old docks. On your *trip around Cartagena's harbour*, you will feel like you are watching a spectacular film → **p. 103**

● *Stretch out on the beach*
Would you prefer a long sandy beach or a small bay to the north or south? You will find it hard to decide where you want to lie down and soak up the sun on the 20km/12mi of coastline in *Dénia* → **p. 71**

INTRODUCTION

DISCOVER THE COSTA BLANCA!

'Here, take this,' says Marisol and pushes a small plate towards her guest, 'you have to try it!' A toothpick pierces the rubbery titbit and lifts it to the man's mouth. 'Now chew it slowly and tell me what you think," the Spanish lady says, watching him expectantly while her husband Antonio greedily spears his third morsel. The taste of the ocean spreads over the palate; it is an unfamiliar but very enjoyable sensation. 'Pulpo seco from here, from Águilas is a real speciality,' Marisol effervesces. She is right. Dried, freshly grilled octopus, served straight out of the pan, is a unique, simply delicious experience and – especially when eaten in a restaurant overlooking the harbour – guaranteed to put you in holiday mood.

Unusual specialities, a thriving gastronomic scene, dream beaches, urban culture, lavish celebrations, a fun nightlife, nature reserves and the traditional stone villages farther inland – there are many good reasons for visiting this coastal region. The

Photo: Benidorm, Platja de Ponent

The town hall square in Valencia is lined with splendid Art Nouveau houses

Sandy beaches and a pulsating metropolis

'White Coast' (Costa Blanca), the 'Hot Coast' (Costa Cálida) and the 'Orange Blossom Coast' (Costa del Azahar) not only have melodious names but also have plenty of surprises, even for those who know Spain well; hidden bays, ports, markets, small taverns and gourmet restaurants. And Valencia, one of the most vibrant cities in the country, is in a league of its own. Spain's eastern Mediterranean coast boasts an enviable climate and is always in season for individual travellers and package tourists. There are hundreds of miles of coastline starting in the Costa del Azahar in the north. This section is part of the Valencian

3rd century BC– 4th century AD
Start of Roman rule after Second Punic War

711
Moors invade the Iberian Peninsula, followed by a flowering of Islam on Spanish territory

1238
Reconquest of Valencia under King Jaume I

1482
Start of construction of the Silk Exchange in Valencia, a symbol of the prosperity of the merchant metropolis

1492
End of the *Reconquista*, the reconquest of the territories occupied by the Moors

province Castelló de la Plana and the Peñíscola and Benicàssim beaches are definite highlights. The beaches around Valencia follow to the south before the 'real' Costa Blanca begins. This is where holiday dreams come true with highlife à la Benidorm, the harbour city Alacant/ Alicante, or more peaceful spots for families with children. Further south, the Costa Blanca runs into the coast of Murcia, which reaches as far as Andalusia with its

> ## A dream holiday: sunshine guaranteed

holiday regions around La Manga de Mar Menor and the Costa Cálida. This section of the coast has some spectacular rocky bays. The area around Murcia also marks a linguistic border. Up to then, Valencian (*Valencià*), a language closely related to Catalan, has been spoken along with normal Spanish (*Castellano),* but in Murcia, *Castellano* once again takes over completely. The inconsistent way the language is dealt with can be somewhat confusing in the Valencian sphere. This can be seen in the different ways town and street names are spelt, which is why this guide often gives two versions of the same name; for example, Alacant is much better known internationally as Alicante.

At least 300 sunny days and 3000 hours of sunshine are the standard every year and, in some regions, rainfall is almost unknown! That is something that emigrants and 'part-time emigrants' from Britain and other countries in Northern and Central Europe value so much. There are many *'residentes'* on the Costa Blanca. The temperature at

1588
Sinking of the Spanish Armada followed by the gradual decline of Spain as a world power

1609
Expulsion of the Christianised Moors, the *moriscos*

1808–14
French invasion

1936–39
Civil war throughout the country, start of dictatorship under Franco

1960s
Economic miracle, introduction of mass tourism with irreparable architectural blunders, especially on the coasts

the height of summer can reach 40°C (104°F) in the deep south of the region around Murcia and Cartagena. The Spaniards usually travel at Easter and in July and August and that is when the area is the liveliest – with all the advantages and disadvantages. If you choose to visit Spain's Mediterranean coast in winter, you will be able to enjoy peace and quiet and be among the privileged few who can eat breakfast on their terrace at the beginning of the year. The average annual temperature around Alacant is 18.5°C (65°F) and a pleasant 13°C (55°F) in January.

Valencia, one of the most beautiful metropolises in Spain, is a good choice for a city trip at any time of the year. The impression made by the beaches and natural beauty spots is complemented by Santiago Calatrava's ultra-modern architecture in the 'City

Valencia, a large city with flair

of the Arts and Sciences' and a more than ample portion of culture. The Valencian Institute of Modern Art and the Museum of Fine Arts have a fine international reputation. The Silk Exchange is a World Heritage Site and the gigantic market

halls opposite have a special charm all of their own. You will feel the flair of the south wherever you go: in the bars, in the parks, on the beaches and in the harbours. The Spaniards use the city's squares and promenades as their second living room – probably in part due to the fact that being invited to a person's home is rather uncommon. The outlook – in spite of all the crises, price increases and press reports about corruption – is generally positive, possibly as a result of the 'mañana' mentality. A popular way to deal with important matters is to put them off until tomorrow: *mañana!* This is not a cliché; it is true, just as it is true that the 'ecological mindset' is still comparatively underdeveloped here.

Culture and nature go hand in hand between the Costa del Azahar and the Murcia coast. The flowering landscapes brim with the exoticism of the Mediterranean. Oranges and lemons, olives, date palms, mimosa, almond and fig trees all flourish under the southern sun. Visitors soon discover that Spain's eastern coast is not only made up of long beaches of fine sand. Small, secluded bays and ruggedly picturesque cliffs are also a common sight. The Sant Antoni and Nao Capes jut out into the sea between Dénia and Calp (Calpe); the coastal mountain ranges, such as El Montgó and Serra d'Irta, are protected by law and there is an impressive mountainous world

1975
End of Francisco Franco's military dictatorship; Juan Carlos named King

1996–2004
Government of the conservative People's Party

2004–11
Socialist government under José Luis Rodríguez Zapatero

2011
Socialists defeated in parliamentary election by the conservative People's Party under Mariano Rajoy; social protests

2012
Severe economic crisis in Spain accompanied by radical austerity measures

in the hinterland. There, the air is full of the aroma of pine trees and herbs; the area near Callosa d'en Sarrià is covered with loquat trees. The white facades of the houses in many villages are made more dazzling by the hibiscus and bougainvillea blossoms; the countryside is carpeted with ice plants, agaves and prickly pear cactuses.

> **The country where the lemons bloom ...**

Over time, the people living here have seen countless foreigners come and go: first Phoenician merchants and sailors, then the Romans, the Moors in the Middle Ages, later pirates from North Africa and Napoleonic troops. In the 1950s, during Franco's dictatorship, Spain started to open itself as a tourist destination and, at the same time, to bury its coastline in an ocean of cement. There are still traces of this unsightly development in cities like Benidorm.

Gem in the hinterland: Old Town and church in Altea

Today, business is booming – and everybody values it as a source of income. Many locals find work in catering, in the hotels and amusement parks. Others do back-breaking work in the commercial ports, oil refineries and brickworks. Work in the orange groves is not an easy option either. Paco, who cultivates a plantation in the hinterland of Dénia, says, 'Some people believe I sit in the sun all day and enjoy the fresh air, but I have 3000 trees here; it's not a hobby, it's hard work from dawn to dusk.' Marisol, who runs a small business in Águilas, also has to work where other people spend their holidays, but she knows how to switch off: traditions such as the daily siesta and a stop for an aperitif at the town bar are sacrosanct. She and Antonio would never change that. Is there anything better than fresh air, the sea and a few pieces of *pulpo seco* ...?

WHAT'S HOT

1 For the stubborn

Donkey A man's best friend is no longer his dog but his donkey. You can find your perfect trekking partner at the donkey protection association *E.S.E.L. e.V. (Parcent, eselcosta blanca.wordpress.com)*. You can also become the sponsor of one of the animals at the farm run by the *Fundación el Burro Patrimonio del Mundo de la Comunitat Valenciana (Cami Les Murtes 17, Jalòn)*. The German-in-exile Gerardo has also actively helped his long-eared friends for years. He is the man committed animal protectors and donkey fans should get in touch with *(gerardo-st.jimdo.com)*.

Fusioned

2

Nouvelle cuisine Spain and the rest of the culinary world have a rendezvous on the Costa Blanca. The Orient adds that special something at *Seu Xerea (C/. Conde de Almodóvar 4, Valencia, www.seuxerea.com, photo)*. Nouvelle cuisine has found a home at *Vuelve Carolina (C/. Correos 8, www.vuelvecarolina.com)*, as well as in *El Bolito*. The latter shows successfully that fusion cooking does not always have to be highly exclusive and terribly expensive *(Plaza de las Flores, Murcia)*.

3 Contemporary

Art There is a fascinating art scene on the Costa. Photography, video, installation – anything goes. Computer graphics and photography join forces in the work of Joël Mestre from Castelló de la Plana *(www.joelmestre.com)*. Creative talents like him receive great support from the galleries: *La Aurora (Plaza de la Aurora 7)* and *Fernando Guerao* in Murcia *(C/. de la Aurora 10)*. *Benlliure* is the right address in Valencia *(C/. Cirilo Amorós 47)*. Angel Mateo Charris is one of the scene's trailblazers *(www. charris.es)*.

Luxury behind old walls

Hotels Mas de Canicatti lies nestled in the middle of an orange grove. The lovingly restored finca and a modern cubistic building now contain 27 rooms as well as the *Orange Spa*, in which citrus fruit are used in the wraps and peelings *(Ctra. de Pedralba, km 2.9, Vilamarxant, photo)*. The walls of the *Casa del Maco* date back to the 18th century but that does not mean you have to forgo any modern comforts in the five double rooms *(Partida Pou Roig 15, Benissa)*. Casa Sibarita opened in an old 19th-century town house. The hotel does without any excessive luxury preferring to give an idea of the typical town houses of the region *(C/. Sant Lluis Gonzaga 40, Rafelguaraf)*.

4

The other side

Benidorm Some people turn up their noses at Benidorm. However, the city with the perfect tourist infrastructure is in the process of reinventing itself. The beaches are no longer just for sunbathing; the *Biblioplaya* means that more is being read there. You can borrow books from a tent *(on the Arenal Bol beach)*. Special events, such as the *Electrobeach* Festival in August, aim at attracting a new class of tourist *(www.electro beachfestival.com, photo)*. Quiet accommodation away from the pulsating centre, such as that provided in the *El Molinet (Partida el Molinet 16, El Castell de Guadalest)* shows that it even possible to get a good night's sleep in the region. The old grain mill is the perfect starting point for hikes in the countryside. The chill-out terrace of the spa-boutique hotel *Villa Venecia* opens up a spectacular view of the sea – and the metamorphosing city *(Plaza San Jaume 1)*.

5

Photo: Orange plantation near Altea

IN A NUTSHELL

ART AND LITERATURE

Francisco Ribalta (1565–1628) and his son Juan Ribalta (1596–1628) are considered the great masters of Valencian Baroque painting and many of their works are on display in the Museu de Belles Arts in Valencia. The city was also the birthplace of an important Impressionist painter Joaquín Sorolla (1863–1923). Among other subjects, his works depict the beach and the fishing villages along the coast of the Levante. The poet Vicente Blasco Ibáñez (1867–1928) was one of Sorolla's contemporaries and it is possible to visit his house – now a museum – in Valencia. Several of his books – including 'The Four Horsemen of the Apocalypse' and 'Blood and Sand' – have been translated into English.

BULLFIGHTING

In spite of many objections and the ban in Catalonia, bullfights *(corridas de toros)* are firmly established in Spain's traditions and will clearly not disappear without difficulty. Toreros are treated like heroes, and their private lives revealed in the yellow press. The new generation is trained in bullfighting schools, yet not all of them make it to the top. Instead of celebrating victories in famous *plazas de toros* like the one in Valencia, many have

On Moors, saints and toreros: all you need to know about a region where legends flourish like the orange trees

to be content with doing the rounds of provincial arenas.

ECONOMY

There are many aspects to Spain's current economic crisis – revealed corruption scandals involving generous presents in the form of tailor-made suits and designer jewellery at the tax payers' expense, foundering banks, bankrupt enterprises, an unemployment rate of more than 20 percent, and mass demonstrations against economic and social policies. The real-estate sector is still very much affected by the crisis and this casts a shadow on the sunny holiday regions. There are hundreds of thousands of empty properties on Spain's coasts; the 'Se vende' sign is omnipresent: 'For Sale!' For years, experts warned that the property bubble would burst but optimists felt that the gold-rush mood would last indefinitely. Short-sightedly, everything that with food processing, but also brick kilns and large manufacturers of all kinds of tiles, stoneware and cement. China pro-

The bullfight – a traditional, but controversial, spectacle

speculation, corruption and the cement mixer made possible was built without giving any consideration to demand. Today, business has become more difficult and many estate agencies have disappeared, but some of the offers are still overpriced. Smart pub owners show how there could be a return to reality with their cheaper 'crisis prices': pure greed has to be put aside. In the meantime, many accommodation providers have also lowered their prices.

If one ignores the times of crisis, one sees a landscape rich in agriculture, with orange groves, artichoke fields, vineyards, and almond and olive orchards. This is all combined with industrial and commercial estates – usually connected duction is another source of work, Elx (Elche) is a shoe-making centre and there are marble-working enterprises in Novelda. The ports of Valencia, Castelló de la Plana and Cartagena are among the busiest commercial shipping centres on the Mediterranean coast: you will not be able to avoid seeing the loading cranes and container terminals. The service sector naturally plays a major role in a region that has focussed on tourism for decades. The annual inflation rate is usually between 2.5 and 4 percent. The low pensions and almost non-existent support for families represent another problem from the Spanish perspective. Spain is quite simply not a welfare state in the traditional sense.

FAUNA

Over time, the massive building activities have driven away many large animals and only smaller species such as foxes, weasels and hedgehogs have managed to survive in nature parks. The bird world is much more diverse with various species of gulls, herons, kingfishers, oystercatchers, peregrine falcons, woodpeckers, swifts, pied avocets and curlews. With a bit of luck, you may even see flamingos and Bonelli's eagles. The reptile kingdom is represented by salamanders, lizards and serpents, including the ladder, grass and Montpellier snakes. There is also a great variety of submarine life: monkfish, conger eel, gilthead sea bream, stingrays and many other species.

FLORA

Although some of the mountains appear bare from a distance, you will discover numerous shrubs and herbs such as rosemary, thyme and Spanish lavender once you get closer. Other Mediterranean flowers found here include juniper, mastic, broom, carob trees, blackthorn, cistus or rock roses, dwarf palms, Kermes oaks and conifers (Mediterranean and Aleppo pines); olive trees and cork oaks are used commercially. Elx's palm grove is so unique that it has been declared a World Heritage Site by the Unesco. Something that is frequently confused with algae and has been washed ashore on some sections of the coast is Neptune grass or Mediterranean tapeweed *Posidonia oceanica*. Meadows of sea grass are proof of high-quality water, offer fish protection and occur in depths of up to 40m (130ft). Information campaigns attempt to increase awareness of the usefulness of these meadows that are frequently damaged by ship anchors and fishing nets.

HEROES AND SAINTS

The Spanish love their heroes and saints. The annual patronal festivals, during which the Virgin Mary or other saints are celebrated, are a fixed part of any calendar. The *Moros y Cristianos* ('Moors and Christians') festivals, with processions, music and gun smoke bring back memories of heroic battles in mediaeval times and victories over the Muslims. The national hero, General El Cid (ca. 1043–1099), was involved in these battles and it was he who first conquered Valencia in 1094. Saint Vincent (Spanish: San Vicente Mártir) died in Valencia in the year 304, centuries before El Cid; according to the legend, he was a victim of the persecution of the Christians under the Roman Emperor Diocletian. Another Saint Vincent

HOW DO I GET TO ...?

Imagine you are in the centre of a town or village looking for a street on the map in your hand. The names there are in Spanish but those on the house walls are in Valencian – not at all unusual in this mixed-language region! In Valencian 'street' is *carrer*; in Spanish, *calle*. There are also different words for 'wide street' (Valencian *avinguda;* Spanish *avenida)* and 'square' *(plaça/plaza)*. In this guide, we use the standard Spanish abbreviations: *C/.* for *Carrer/Calle*, *Av.* for *Avinguda/Avenida*, *Pl.* for *Plaça/playa* and *s/n* for *sin numero* 'without a house number'.

was born in Valencia: San Vicente Ferrer (ca. 1350–1419) was a member of the Dominican order and active as a preacher of repentance. And, of course: there are those who believe that the 'Holy Grail' can be worshipped in Valencia Cathedral.

LANGUAGE

The spread, acceptance and use of language as an expression of regional identity is something of a problem in multilingual Spain. 'High Spanish' *Castellano* is the most common but Galician *(Galego)*, Basque *(Euskera)* and *Catalan (Català)* are officially recognised throughout the country. This is not the case with Valencian *(Valencià)*, which is very similar to Catalan, and consequently the cause of bitter political disputes. From the Valencian viewpoint, *Valencià* is an independent language whereas the Catalans regard *Valencià* as a special form of *Català*. But, *Valencià* is recognised on the regional level and widely spoken from the Costa del Azahar to the southern fringes of the Costa Blanca.

MODERN ARCHITECTURE

Valencia is proud of being the home to one of the major flagships of modern architecture in Spain: the sensational futuristic ensemble of the 'City of Arts and Sciences' *(Ciutat de les Arts i les Ciènces)* that covers an area of 86 acres. One of the buildings in the complex, the *Oceanogràfic* was designed by Félix Candela but there is no mistaking the signature of Santiago Calatrava on the dazzling white *Hemisfèric*, the *Museu de les Ciències Príncipe Felipe* and the *Palau des Arts Reina Sofía*. The architect was born in Valencia in 1951, and his buildings are characterised by their large clear structures and forms. But Calatrava is not without his critics: the longer it took to complete construction of his final creation for the Ciutat, *El Ágora* (which lasted until 2012), the more the costs exceeded the initial calculations and the more the architect earned. This led to negative headlines in the press. In these times of crisis, Spain reacts hypersensitively to such matters … Valencia's music palace, *Palau de la Música*, was planned by José María García de Parades, winner of the National Architecture Prize. Another prominent Spanish architect, Ricardo Bofill, designed the *Aigüera Park* in Benidorm and a labyrinthine building complex in the La Manzanera district in Calp.

POLITICAL STRUCTURE

Spain has a population of around 47 million and is divided into 17 *Comunidades Autónomas*, autonomous communities that can be compared with the states of the USA. This guide deals with the autonomous communities of Valencia (9000mi²; with the provinces of Valencia Castelló de la Plana and Alacant) and Murcia (4360mi²). Murcia is one of the few autonomous communities not divided into individual provinces.

POPULATION

With only a few exceptions, the entire coastline is relatively densely populated. Valencia (pop. 800,000) is far and away the largest city, followed by Alacant (320,000), Cartagena (215,000) and Castelló de la Plana (150,000). The main cities in the hinterland are Murcia (350,000) and Elx (220,000). Today, not only Spaniards live in this part of Spain. The economic boom shortly before the turn of the millennium, along with the demand for labour and the effects of the low birth rate in the country, led to an influx of immigrants from Latin America and North and Sub-Saharan Africa. In the meantime, the continuing effects of the

Spanish economic crisis have not only slowed down this movement but also caused quite a few non-European immigrants to leave the country. There are also 'immigrants' of a different kind in the region around Dénia and Calp. A large British resident community, consisting of people who are still actively employed (as doctors, lawyers, authors, etc) or simply want to enjoy their retirement under the southern sun has established itself in the area. It is now estimated that there is a total of several hundred thousand old-age pensioners and residents who live more or less regularly on the coasts.

mainly in the south and east but were soon confronted with resistance from the *Reconquista* 'Christian reconquest'. This was finally successful and the last Moorish realm in Granada fell in 1492. Traces of the

Moors and Christians shoulder to shoulder

RECONQUISTA

In the year 711, the Moorish army took advantage of the strife in the Visigoth realm to cross over the Straits of Gibraltar from North Africa and invade the Iberian Peninsula. They established themselves

Moors can still be seen in the architecture of the country (castles, palaces), numerous place names – those starting with 'beni' or 'al-' – and sophisticated forms of agricultural irrigation.

SPORTS CRAZE

Football reigns supreme in the country that is currently World Champion. And it is no different in this region! The traditional Valencia C.F. was Spanish champion once and C.F. Villareal has been very successful in recent years, qualifying itself for the Champions League. But once a year, footballs have to make way for tyres when the cars in the elite class of Formula 1 racing roar around the course in Valencia.

FOOD & DRINK

If there is one thing the Spanish do not save on, it is creature comforts. Eating and drinking are high on their list of priorities and plenty of time is taken to enjoy them – regardless of whether the meal is held in the company of colleagues from work and friends or just with the family.

A main meal can easily last two or three hours. The several courses are usually followed with coffee and liqueur or brandy. By contrast, breakfast *(desayuno)*, taken around 8am, is fairly simple and – in terms of quality and quantity – cannot be compared with lunch and especially not with dinner: Early in the morning, Spaniards like it sweet and simple: milk

coffee *(café con leche)* and maybe a croissant; they save the real eating for later on! And that means tapas – all kinds of titbits – that people like to eat to whet their appetite for lunch *(comida)*. This usually starts at around 1.30 or 2pm while, as a rule, dinner *(cena)* is not until 9 or 9.30pm at the earliest. To accommodate those tourists who are not used to this rhythm, most restaurants in the holiday resorts start serving much earlier. And many hotels have also adapted their breakfast buffets to meet the requirements of their guests.

The reduced supply and resulting increase in prices means that fish has become

Photo: Tapas

From paella to almond milk – frugal breakfast, tapas between meals and the art of dining for hours in the evening

quite expensive. The most popular varieties include sea bass *(lubina)*, monkfish *(rape)*, sea snails *(caracoles de mar)*, octopus *(pulpo)* and small squid *(chipirones)*. And, of course, paella is a standard; but there can be great differences in the quality of this rice dish. Unfortunately, many tourist restaurants serve rice with cheap fish stock as 'authentic paella'. In a good paella, it should be possible to recognise and taste all of the individual ingredients, from the vegetables (tomatoes, peppers, etc.) to the seafood (squid, mussels, etc.) and meat (pork, chicken, lamb or rabbit), depending on the variety chosen.

Although there are simple one-course 'mixed platters' *(platos combinados)* on the menu and a serving of potato omelette *(tortilla de patata)* can really fill you up, Spaniards are much more accustomed to

LOCAL SPECIALITIES

▶ **arròs a banda/arroz a banda** – a rice dish cooked in fish broth

▶ **arròs negre/arroz negro** – rice with squid and its ink; literally translated: 'black rice' botifarra/butifarra – pork sausage, cold or hot, in black and white varieties *(butifarra negra or blanca)*

▶ **caldero** – rice dish with the broth of various types of seafood and fish

▶ **chorizo** – hearty pork sausage with paprika and garlic; can be eaten raw or cooked in stews

▶ **chulitas de cordero lechal** – lamb chops; frequently grilled *(a la plancha)*

▶ **cruet de peix** – fish stew, popular in the region of Xábia

▶ **fideuá** – a slightly different version of paella made with soup noodles *(fideos)* instead of rice

▶ **gambas** – shrimp, often grilled *(gambas a la plancha)* or in garlic and oil *(gambas al ajillo)*

▶ **horchata** – sweet tiger-nut milk, drunk ice-cold (photo right)

▶ **langostinos** – large shrimp; the fresh *langostinos* from Peñíscola are especially good (and, unfortunately, correspondingly expensive)

▶ **mariscada** – mixed seafood platter with shrimp and prawns and often crayfish *(cigalas)* and razor clams *(navajas)*

▶ **nísperos** – loquats, most common in the hinterland of Benidorm and Calp; the aromatic fruit are preserved in syrup *(nísperos en almíbar)* or processed as loquat honey *(miel de níspero),* loquat nectar *(nectar de níspero),* loquat jam *(mermelada de níspero)* and loquat schnapps *(aguardiente de níspero)*

▶ **paella** – this rice dish is the perennial classic of Spanish Mediterranean cooking: many variations of paella – the yellow colour comes from saffron (or curcuma) – are served in the region including paella with seafood *(paella de mariscos, paella marinera)* and mixed paella *(paella mixta)* with fish and meat (usually chicken). (Photo left)

▶ **pescado en escabeche** – fish – tuna, for example – in (orange) marinade

▶ **pulpo seco** – dried octopus, cooked on the griddle

having several courses. The three-course menu of the day *(menu del día)* served in local restaurants on workdays is usually more than satisfactory and the price from around 9 or 10 euros includes a glass of wine. This will probably not be a culinary revelation but good, honest cooking of an acceptable quality with tasty dishes. Just make sure that the restaurant owner does not try to charge extra for the wine, even though it is included, or for other things you did not eat. There is the occasional black sheep. Sometimes just requesting the complaint form *(hoja de reclamación)*, which every bar and restaurant is required to have by law, can work wonders ...

The Spanish like to share a platter *(tablas; a cheese platter is a plata de quesos)* or have small portions of food (*raciones*; a portion of mussels is a *ración de mejillones)* to start their meal. The more exclusive restaurants often serve a 'tasting menu' *(menu de degustación)* in which the chef shows off his talents by serving small helpings of a variety of dishes. However, you must expect to pay at least 30 euros per person for this pleasure, and a really good *menu de degustación* can easily cost twice this amount – without wine. By the way, it is customary to wait to be seated – not only in top restaurants!

Spaniards like sweet things – not only for breakfast. The high sugar content of some of the desserts and cakes might seem too sweet for visitors from other parts of Europe. Alacant and Xixona are the home of *turrones* the traditional almond and honey blocks that are an essential part of any Spanish Christmas feast. There are many variations – from smooth and creamy to nutty and hard. The oranges grown on the plantations in the region are used to produce juice or sold to be eaten.

The Spaniards place great value on their solid or liquid nourishment being home- or hand-made *(casero, artesano)*. ●

INSIDER TIP La Casa del Papa Luna *(C/. Mayor 33 | www.lacasadelpapaluna.com)*,

a shop in the Old Town of Peñíscola, sells wonderful homemade vermouth *(vermouth casero)* and kola-nut liqueur *(licor de nuez de kola)* under the 'Papa Luna' label. The family has produced this fine tipple from the African kola nut on the Costa del Azahar since 1894. A super-sweet concoction, the herb liquor '43', which is famous throughout Spain, is produced in Cartagena.

Exquisite: monkfish with shrimps

In the wine-growing country Spain, the Valencia and Alacant cultivation areas have a protected designation of origin *(Denominación de Origen,* or DO for short). A little further inland, the Utiel-Requena, Yecla and Jumilla areas produce high-quality DO red wines. Beer is a popular drink in the *cervecerías* with *San Miguel* and *Mahou* among the most popular brands.

SHOPPING

There are more shops than one can count here – but just as many shoddy goods Made in China or India. The shopping districts in a city like Benidorm resemble gigantic warehouses of Asian products with a monstrous selection of bags, t-shirts and bric-a-brac. This deluge of mass-produced articles might make it difficult for you to recognise real quality when you see it, but these shopping zones are at least full of life.

ARTS AND CRAFTS

Ceramics have always been a popular souvenir. There are pottery shops in Peñíscola that sell handmade jugs and vases with unique designs; you will also find what you are looking for near Alacant and Agost. The cork jugs with metal ornaments made in the area around Sagunt make decorative souvenirs. Depending on whether they are intended to lie or stand, they are known either as a *colcho* or *colcha*.

CULINARY SPECIALITIES

You will be able to buy products to satisfy sophisticated palates from the producer in many towns and villages: liqueur and dessert wines in Benicassìm and almond-and-honey sweets *(turrones)* in Xixona. Glasses of preserved capers *(alcaparras)* are a speciality of Águilas. Supermarkets are the places to buy inexpensive bottles or tins of good olives *(aceitunas)* and cold-pressed olive oil *(aceite de oliva virgin extra)* – always good value for money. Buying bottles of olive oil or wine only really makes sense for those who have travelled to Spain in a car, since airports have strict regulations concerning transporting liquids in your carry-on luggage. A broken bottle of oil or wine in the suitcase could put a damper on the fun you had shopping. *Chorizos,* hard sausages with paprika and garlic, are delicious and easy to transport. An even better idea is to have sausages and cheese shrink-wrapped *(envasar al vacío)*. You should buy some high-quality Serrano ham – it is two to three times less expensive than at home.

FASHION

The many boutiques and shoe shops, with a range of goods from chic to down-to-

> You will find plenty to take your fancy but there is a lot of junk, so you need to keep your eyes open for the quality products!

earth, make Valencia a good place to go shopping. But you should also pay attention to quality here; you will not be happy with your leather sandals for 20 euros if the straps rip after only a few days! You should expect good brand-name leather shoes to cost at least 60–70 euros. The *El Corte Inglés* chain of department stores offers those looking for quality all they need under a single roof. The young fashion sold by chains such as *Zara* and *Mango* targets the less affluent.

MARKETS

The *rastros* and *mercadillos*, street markets with all kinds of goods, are held on regular days in many villages and are very popular. Clothing is a major attraction, but cheap does not necessarily mean that you really save money. You should look closely before you buy. It can be very lively at the normal weekly markets *(mercados)* and they are usually good places to buy fruit and vegetables as well as the typical products of the region such as cheese, honey, wine and olive oil. The market halls are usually open Mon–Sat 8am–2pm; the fish section is closed on Monday. Valencia has one of the largest and most beautiful market halls in all of Spain – opposite the Silk Exchange.

MUSIC

It might be a cliché – but the Spanish have rhythm in their blood. And, they also like to listen to pop and rock in their own language. David Bisbal, Estopa, Amaral, Juanes and La Oreja de van Gogh are just some of the performers storming the charts. The music departments of the *El Corte Inglés* chain have a wide range of CDs.

THE PERFECT ROUTE

LEAD-UP TO THE COAST

The route is conceived as a round trip from and to Valencia and invites motorists to discover all the coast and hinterland has to offer. The main focus is on the Costa Blanca. The starting point is the airport at ① *Valencia* → p. 44 where you collect the hired car that you booked in advance. You can put off visiting the city itself until after you return. After you leave the airport, take the ring road to the south and drive on the motorway until you reach the exit to ② *Dénia* → p. 69. You should plan to spend two nights here in what is one of the most delightful little towns on the Costa Blanca. The castle, the beaches and the marina in Dénia offer a fascinating cultural mix.

ON THE PROMONTORY AND IN THE MOUNTAINS

Dénia is the ideal starting point for a full-day excursion to ③ *Cap de la Nao* → p. 72 and ④ *Calp* → p. 67 with its beaches and the famous rocky landmark *Penyal d'Ifac* (photo right). The picturesque mountain village of ⑤ *Guadalest* → p. 66, poetry in stone, despite the many visitors, lies waiting for you near Calp. Back in Dénia, you will still have time to freshen up with a dip in the hotel pool or the sea before you go to dinner. *Chimichurri* is a popular restaurant at the marina specialising in tasty grilled food.

OFF TO ALACANT!

The next day, you can cover the stretch from Dénia to the port city of Alacant, which is better known under its Spanish name of Alicante, in one go unless you want to make a stopover in the lively holiday resort ⑥ *Benidorm* → p. 62. Instead of looking for rooms directly in the city of ⑦ *Alacant* → p. 56, it is better to spend the night away from the main centre near the beach area at *Platja de Sant Joan*. You must visit the castle, the *Castillo de Santa Bárbara*, in Alacant. Then you can set off to explore the old city and harbour area of Alacant – or just relax on the *Platja de Sant Joan*; tomorrow you have a long drive ahead of you to get know the southern section of your destination: **8** *La Manga del Mar Menor* → p. 83 on the inland sea the Mar Menor 'Little Sea'. It is worth spending two nights there so that you have enough time to explore the **9** *Cabo de Palos* → p. 84 and make a short trip to **10** *Cartagena* → p. 87, the harbour town in the south-west.

PALM GROVES, MOORS AND CHRISTIANS

The motorway makes it easy to get around quickly and you drive back over the AP7 to the north after you leave La Manga del Mar Menor and head for **11** *Elx (Elche)* → p. 73, the city of palms. The highlight is a foray into the palm groves of the *Huerto del Cura*. Maybe you would like to spend the night here before driving north-east into the hinterland and making a stopover in **12** *Alcoi (Alcoy)* → p. 64. You should visit the town's historical centre and admire the Art Nouveau architecture. Alcoi becomes really packed in April and May when it is invaded by hordes of

Moors and Christians for the *Moros y Cristianos* festival. The barren, mountainous surroundings of Alcoi give way to more fertile land farther to the north. The small mountain town of **13** *Xàtiva (Játiva)* → p. 55 is a pleasant place to spend the last night of your road tour.

THE METROPOLIS

The A7 takes you from Xàtiva through a fertile, hill-lined valley full of orange groves back to the starting point in **14** *Valencia* (photo, far left). This marks the end of the 'Perfect Route'. It is not worth keeping the car in town. After returning it to the rental company, you should plan on spending at least two or three days in Valencia to experience all the charm and vitality of the city.

Approx. 750km (466mi)
Driving time: approx. 15 hours;
recommended travel time: 8 days
Detailed map of the route on the back cover, in the road atlas and the pull-out map

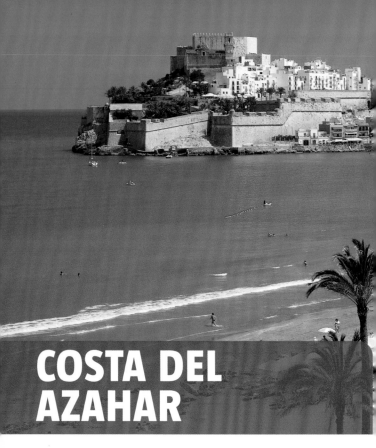

COSTA DEL AZAHAR

The 'Orange Blossom Coast', Costa del Azahar, lives up to its name. In spring, the flowering trees exude a bewitching perfume, and much of the landscape is dominated by plantations. Olives, almonds and artichokes add to the exotic and breathtaking scenery.

This sun-flooded stretch of the coast has all the ingredients for a perfect holiday: a bountiful supply of seafood in the restaurants, fishing ports and beaches, enchanting towns such as Peñíscola, caves and traditional villages in the hinterland, nature reserves such as the Serra d'Irta and Desert de les Palmes. While some other areas along the Mediterranean coast have become buried beneath rows of concrete hotels, the around 120km (75mi)-long Costa del Azahar has remained comparatively unexplored territory. Discovering the surroundings and staying in traditional accommodation in the countryside in villages like Vilafamés is an attractive alternative. You will be amazed!

BENICÀSSIM/ BENICASIM

(123 E4) (*M F4*) **The somewhat strange-sounding name of this small town (pop.**

A play of colour wherever you look: golden yellow beaches, blue sea, green parks and the dazzling oranges in the fruit plantations

16,000), which covers a wide area approx. 80km (50mi) north of Valencia, comes from its Arabic origin; the Moors and Christians waged many violent battles in this area between the 11th and 13th centuries.

In later centuries, the coast was subject to attack by pirates; the watchtower from the 16th century behind the Platja Torre Sant Vicent was once part of an extensive defence system with almost twenty similar towers.

Starting at the end of the 19th century, well-off Valencians became the next to lay siege to Benicàssim – they were the forerunners of modern-day tourists and had magnificent villas built behind the beaches where they idled away their long summers. This developed into the 'Valencian Biarritz'. The wide sandy beaches and

Sunbathing at the Platja Heliópolis in Benicàssim

pleasant climate are still the main assets of Benicàssim and the historical villas are now listed as protected buildings.

SIGHTSEEING

BODEGAS CARMELITANO ⭐

The production of these tasty tipples including the famous *licor carmelitano* can be traced back to the Carmelite monks who established the monastery in Benicàssim at the beginning of the 18th century. It is made of a carefully guarded 'miracle recipe' consisting of around 40 different herbs. Visitors taking part in the ● tours of the time-honoured cellars, distillery and bottling plant will be almost overpowered by the sweetish aroma. Nowadays, the operation is no longer run by the monks but by normal workers. Some of the massive oak barrels can contain 4000 litres (880 gallons). The current

entrance fee of 2.50 euros includes a INSIDER TIP sample at the end of the tour. You will be able to try the sweet 'communion wine', muscatel, and apple, hazelnut and Carmelite liqueurs. The shop sells the entire range of products at reasonable prices. *C/. Bodolz 12 | daily 9am–1.30pm and 3–6.30pm (in summer 3.30–7.30pm) | www.carmelitano.com*

FOOD & DRINK

CASA VICENTE

This restaurant is very popular with the locals, especially for its INSIDER TIP exceptionally low-priced daily set menus. The paella is also delicious. *Closed Sat | Plaça La Estación 8 | tel. 9 64 30 12 49 | Budget*

MESÓN LA ESTAFETA

Elegant ambience with a rustic interior decorated with a lot of wood; near the centre. The house specialises in typical Mediterranean cuisine with the main focus on rice dishes. *Closed Sun evening and Mon | Paseo Pérez Bayer 35 | tel. 9 64 30 21 81 | www.mesonestafeta.com | Moderate*

BEACHES

The most beautiful ⭐ beaches in Benicàssim start on the coastal road Santa Maria del Mar and are separated from each other by artificial moles: *Platja Voramar, Platja Almadrava* and *Platja Torre San Vicent.* The beaches are wide and covered with fine sand with magnificent promenades running parallel to them. The smaller *Platja Els Terrers* and the long *Platja Heliópolis* continue farther to the south but here the view is impaired by the ugly skyline of the commercial port of Castelló de la Plana. Our tip is to keep as far away as possible!

SPORTS & ACTIVITIES

In summer, water lovers are drawn to the large pool landscapes of the *Aquarama (Ctra. N-340, km 986.8 | mid-June–beginning of Sept daily 11am–7pm | www.aquarama.net)* aquatic park with its many slides, a tropical wave pool and other attractions. There is a total of 15km (9mi) of cycle lanes in Benicàssim. The INSIDER TIP short tour along the 'Green Route' (Vía Verde) to Oropesa del Mar is very beautiful. Bicycle hire: see 'Low Budget' box on p. 43.

ENTERTAINMENT

The most popular inns and pubs where people meet to spend the long evening hours are along the central streets – Avenida da Castelló and Avenida Santo Tomás – as well as behind the Platja Sant Vicent and the Plaça dels Dolors (e.g.

La Lluna | Nr. 32 | www.puntcastello.es/lalluna).

WHERE TO STAY

MONTREAL
Functional three-star house with an outdoor pool. The optional extra price for full or half board is good value for money. In summer, the minimum stay is one week (otherwise, a supplement is charged). *70 rooms | C/. Les Barraques 5 |*

⭐ **Bodegas Carmelitano**
In the realm of sweet wines and liqueurs – samples included!
→ p. 34

⭐ **Beaches at Benicàssim**
Sandy capital for turnover on the promenade – the most beautiful beaches are: Voramar, Almadrava and Torre Sant Vicent → p. 35

⭐ **Desert de les Palmes/Desierto de las Palmas**
The rugged mountain world behind Benicàssim → p. 37

⭐ **Vilafamés**
Unspoilt village in the hinterland with castle ruins and rural accommodation → p. 38

⭐ **Old town in Peñíscola**
The walled district on the way up towards the castle still exudes a village atmosphere → p. 38

⭐ **Serra d'Irta Nature Reserve**
Cliffs, beaches, hiking paths and marvellous views south of Peñíscola → p. 42

MARCO POLO HIGHLIGHTS

tel. 9 64 30 06 81 | www.hotelmontreal.
es | *Moderate*

TERMAS MARÍNAS EL PALASIET

Four-star spa hotel; however, somewhat
out of town. This is where fans of relaxing
thalasso therapy treatments will feel at
home. Various packages lasting several
days including accommodation, board
and spa facilities. *74 rooms | Pontazgo 11 |
tel. 9 64 30 02 50 | www.palasiet.com |
Expensive*

TRAMONTANA

Strategically favourable location behind
the Platja Torre Sant Vicent only a short
walk from the beach and promenade. The
strung-out house has two stars. *Closed in
winter | 65 rooms | Paseo Marítimo
Ferrandis Salvador 6 | tel. 9 64 30 03 00 |
www.hoteltramontana.com | Budget*

INFORMATION

C/. Santo Tomás 76-bajo | tel. 9 64 30
01 02 | www.turismobenicassim.com

WHERE TO GO

CASTELLÓ DE LA PLANA/CASTELLÓN DE LA PLANA (123 E4) (ഝ F4)

In the middle of the 13th century, it was
decided to move the city from the nearby
mountain slopes down to the coastal plain
La Plana. This historical event is celebrated
every year in March (sometimes continuing into April) at the colourful *Fiestas de
la Magdelena* with processions, firework
displays and bullfights. However, there are
not many buildings of historical interest
in this provincial capital (pop. 150,000)
12km (7.5mi) south of Benicàssim. There
is the 17th-century bell tower of the *Con-
catredral de Santa María*, but the *market
halls* not far away, with their fish, sausage
and cheese sections are actually much
more interesting. The theatre is the cultural centre of the town and there is a
spiritual highlight just outside the city – the
*Basílica de Santa María del Lledo (daily,
depending on mass times and weddings)*;
the chapel dates from the late Middle Ages.
The port of *El Grao*, a few miles to the east

Fishermen unload their catch at El Grao port in Castelló

of the city centre, is also part of Castelló de la Plana. The *Planetarium (Passeig Marítim 1 | Tue–Sun changing opening times)* looms up out of the not exactly edifying panorama. In addition, trips to the Columbretes Islands depart from the harbour. Information: *Tourist office | Pl. Maria Agustina 5 | tel. 9 64 35 86 88 | www.castello. es (city) | www.castellon-costaazahar.com (province)*

DESERT DE LES PALMES/
DESIERTO DE LAS PALMAS ★
(123 E3) (*Ø F–G4*)

The name of this nature reserve that rises up to a height of 729m (2392ft) can be translated as the 'Palm Desert. In a figurative sense, 'desert' symbolises the solitude the Carmelite monks withdrew to centuries ago. The monastery we see today dates from the 18th century and is located on a lovely mountain road; signposted from Benicàssim. After you leave the railway and motorway behind you, you drive up the curving CV-147 country road into the mountains; this route is also very popular with cyclists. Common plants in the area are pines, arbutus and various hard herbs including rosemary and thyme. Along the way, there are several places where you can park you car 🍴 and admire the splendid panoramic views of the Mediterranean and over to Benicàssim. The monks open their small museum after midday mass on Sunday but are not always as friendly as you would expect! A spiritual centre is also part of the complex. A hike to the castle on a rock *Montornés (starting point directly on the road)* is another interesting activity in the mountains. *www.desiertodelaspalmas.com*

ILLES COLUMBRETES/
ISLAS COLUMBRETES (0) (*Ø H4–5*)

This archipelago around 30 sea miles off the coast was created by volcanic activity.

The rugged island world is protected by law and is a popular destination for boat trips and diving excursions – depending on the weather and season. The busiest starting point for these tours is the port in Castelló de la Plana, with *Golodrina Clavel (Muelle de Costa | tel. 9 64 48 08 06)* and other operators.

ORPRESA/OROPESA DEL MAR
(123 E3) (*Ø F–G4*)

The small village (pop. 8000) 10km (6mi) to the north-east is divided into three sections: the Old Town, the coastal village and the Marina d'Or holiday village. The remains of the castle in the Old Town can be visited, free of charge, during the day. Its origins can be traced back to Muslim rule and it was also in the hands of the Knights Hospitaller in the Middle Ages. The Chapel of Mary *Virgen de la Paciencia* (18th century), the *Museo del Naipe (C/. Hospital 1 | daily 10.30am–1.30pm and 5.30–8pm | www.museodelnaipe.com)* with its collection of playing cards and the artistic wrought-iron objects in the *Museo del Hierro (C/. Ramón y Cajal/Sorolla | Mon– Fri 10am–2pm)* are also worth visiting.

The most beautiful beach is the sweeping, shell-shaped *Platja de la Concha* and it is also the prime location of the *Hotel Marina (17 rooms | Paseo Marítimo La Concha 12 | tel. 9 64 31 00 99 | www.hotel marina.com.es | Moderate);* the restaurant is also popular with people not staying at the hotel. The marina is at the southern end of Platja de la Concha while a path in the opposite direction leads past the lighthouse promontory to the *Morro de Gos* and *Les Amplàries* beaches as well as the coastal monster *Marina d'Or* with all of its architectural eyesores. *Marina d'Or* even boasts that it is the 'largest leisure and holiday city in Europe'. This might be a blatant exaggeration but there are certainly more than enough sparkling lights, kitsch and hullabaloo. This is where you can find hotels and health complexes, holiday flats, a park for children, restaurants, bars and discos. Gardens are laid out in neo-modernist style and footbridges lead down to the beach. Of course, there are also all kinds of events.

Information: *Tourist office | Pl. París | tel. 9 64 31 23 20 | www.oropesadelmar.es*

VILAFAMÉS ⭐
(123 E3) *(⏍ F4)*

This hamlet (pop. 1500) around 25km (16mi) from Benicàssim is one of the most beautiful places in the hinterland of the Costa del Azahar. Vilafamés is built several ledges on the slopes, and there is a spectacular panoramic view ⬧⬧ from the highest point by the (freely accessible) castle ruins. You should park your car in the lower section of the village or at the open car park in front of the Assumpció Renaissance church. Narrow streets with quarry-stone buildings and hanging plants are set off against the whitewashed facades of the houses in the village. The simple *Hotel El Rullo (6 rooms | C/. La Fuente 2 | tel. 9 64 32 93 84 | Budget)* is a centrally located place to stay. The hotel also has a down-to-earth rustic restaurant with a choice of two daily set menus *(daily | Budget–Moderate)*. A little farther away, the same management also runs the somewhat more expensive, but still affordable, *El Antic Portal (11 rooms | tel. 9 64 32 93 84 | www.anticportal.com | Budget–Moderate)*. And that is just as good an address for a local countryside hotel as the INSIDER TIP ▶ *El Jardin Vertical*, a rustic-style building with elements from the 16th century *(8 rooms | C/. Nou 15 | tel. 9 64 32 99 38 | www.eljardinvertical. com | Moderate | bookings also over the Rusticae country hotel chain: www.rusticae. es). www.vilafames.es*

PEÑÍSCOLA

(123 F2) *(⏍ G3)* **Affording a unique view of the entire coast of the Mediterranean, the fortified old-town promontory of Peñíscola (pop. 5000) juts out into the sea high above the harbour and beaches.** Square, whitewashed houses are staggered up to the highest plateau of the rocky hillock, which is dominated by a mediaeval fortress. The newly constructed areas of the city spread out away from the historical heart of Peñíscola. Sand filling made it possible to extend the North Beach as far as the neighbouring village of Benicarló; palm-lined promenades invite visitors to take long strolls in their shade. The small pond landscape in the centre of the busy new city is another cheerful sight: with ducks, eucalyptus trees and playground facilities for the children. Many Spanish families enjoy spending their holidays in Peñíscola.

SIGHTSEEING

OLD TOWN ⭐ ● ⬧⬧

Peñíscola claims to have the most beautiful Old Town on the entire Costa del Azahar: the 16th-century walls surround a mountain spur. Visitors are swallowed up by the *Portal de Sant Pere,* a city gate with the C/. Atarazanas rising up behind it. This is where you will find the blowhole that fizzes and hisses and sprays when there are high waves and rough seas. You make your way upwards over warped paving through a complex system of narrow lanes. The C/. Nou will overwhelm you with its lush floral glory; in the distance, you will catch a glimpse of the sea; small bars and restaurants line the way. The castle and small lighthouse occupy the highest point at around 65m (213ft). One leaves or enters the Old Town from the North Beach side through the steep *Subida Portal Fosc.*

CASTLE

This fortress with its battlements was erected by the Knights Templar between 1294 and 1307 on the site of a former Moorish complex. At the time of the so-called 'Western Schism', the splitting of the church that lasted from 1378 to 1417, Pope Benedict XIII sought refuge in the castle at Peñíscola. His real name was Pedro de Luna; he came from Aragon and was ultimately unsuccessful in his attempt to take over control of the Catholic Church. He managed to survive many attempts made to poison him before dying at around 80 years of age in 1423. His body was temporarily entombed in the castle church and the bare room he died in can be visited. The castle is also known as 'Papa Luna' in honour of its most famous resident; the labyrinthine complex, which even includes a dungeon, has been pains-takingly restored. There are magnificent views over the beaches and mountains from the ☆ esplanade and upper lookout platform. *Pl. de Armas | daily 10.30am–5.30pm, in summer, daily 9.30am–9.30pm*

FISHING PORT ☆

The fishing port *(puerto pesquero)* is an inviting place to take a stroll along the moles and opens up splendid views of the hills in the background and walled castle in the Old Town. In addition, an exceed-ingly busy fishing fleet has its home here. Depending on the season, weather and success of the catch, the fishermen come back to port between 4 and 5pm from Monday to Friday and that is when the fish auction begins. Visitors can watch them unloading their boats and get a glance at what goes on at the auction, which is not open to the general public, through the large window fronts of the

The coastline is lined with palm trees in Peñíscola

long *Llotja de peix* building. The *Bar Puerto Mar* is a good place to relax over a cup of coffee.

MUSEU DE LA MAR

Small maritime museum in an old-town building that was once used as the village school. Information and exhibits about fishing and the local port. *In summer, daily 10am–2pm and 5–9pm, at other* times, daily 10am–2pm and 4–8pm | entrance free | C/. Princep s/n

FOOD & DRINK

INSIDER TIP **CASA DOROTEA**

This restaurant is the place to go in the Old Town for a good meal in an informal

HOGAR DEL PESCADOR

Heaven for people who love eating fish and seafood. In spite of the simple décor, however, the Hogar serves upmarket food that is not exactly inexpensive. Located near the fishing port. *Daily | Llotja Vella s/n | tel. 9 64 48 95 88 | Moderate–Expensive*

Peace returns to the beach at Peñíscola after the sun worshipers leave

ambience: the speciality of the house is the excellent paella. There are also a few tables and chairs outside on the pavement. Simple but authentic. *Closed Tue | C/. San Vicente 12 | tel. 9 64 48 08 63 | Budget–Moderate*

EL CID

On the busiest street in the centre of town; a good selection ranging from black rice to a mixed fish platter. Popular with the locals. If it is too full for you, there are plenty of alternatives nearby. *Daily | Av. España 32 | tel. 9 64 48 06 40 | Moderate*

SHOPPING

INSIDER TIP **FRUTAS PIÑANA** ●

A gigantic shop with freshly harvested fruit and vegetables and the best prices far and wide. Ideal for those who are catering for themselves or have driven here and want to take a crate of oranges back home with them. *Av. Papa Luna 116 | the car park can only be reached from the rear*

BEACHES

The main area is the *Playa Norte* (North Beach); it stretches for miles and is well provided with showers, children's playground equipment and beach-volleyball nets. The small *Playa Sur* (South Beach) near the fishing port is actually rather large but cannot be recommended for swimming.

SPORTS & ACTIVITIES

The long beach promenade towards Benicarló is very popular with joggers. There is also a lane for cyclists (a rather rare occurrence in Spain); bikes can be hired from *Bicicletas Freddy (Av. Papa Luna 79 | Edificio Marina)*, *Diver-Sport (Av. Estación 17 | tel. 9 64 48 20 06)* and elsewhere. In the high season, excursion boats set sail regularly for half-hour trips around the promontory. The *Acualandia (Av. Papa Luna | Urbanización Peñismar II)* water park is usually open from the beginning of June until the end of September and is a real hit with children.

ENTERTAINMENT

Things can become rather lively on the promenade near the North Beach and in the area around the main street Av. España. However, Peñíscola is more of a destination for families and therefore does not have a great choice of nightlife. One exception is the *Fleca* disco *(Plaza Ayuntamiento s/n)*.

WHERE TO STAY

APARTHOTEL JARDINES DEL PLAZA

Pleasantly furnished holiday flats, well suited for families. Split-level, with a small kitchen on the lower floor. The beach is just across the promenade; check-in in the neighbouring hotel *Peñíscola Plaza Suites*. 130 flats | Av. Papa Luna 156 | tel. 9 64 01 07 00 | www.zthotels.net | *Moderate*

CAMPING EDÉN

This camping site with a swimming pool area and restaurant near the beach is open throughout the year and also rents out simple wooden huts and cottages. *Carretera CS-501 Peñíscola–Benicarló, km 6 | tel. 9 64 48 05 62 | www.camping-eden.com | Budget*

GRAN HOTEL PEÑÍSCOLA

This is definitely the best of the hotels near the beach: four stars and spacious rooms. On the lower level, there is an indoor swimming pool and spa offering various rejuvenating packages. A supplement is charged for rooms with a view of the sea; car parking space is available. As a rule, room prices are based on either half or full board. *437 rooms | Av. Papa Luna 136 | tel. 9 64 46 90 06 | www.granhotelpeniscola.com | Expensive*

INFORMATION

Paseo Marítimo s/n | tel. 9 64 48 02 08 | www.peniscola.es

WHERE TO GO

ALCOSSEBRE/ALCOCEBRE

(123 F3) (*ФД* G3)
Coastal community (pop. 6000) spread out over a wide area with white houses, a marina, pedestrian-friendly promenades and a lovely view towards the Serra d'Irta Nature Park. The most beautiful beaches – *Romana, Cargador* and *Las Fuentes* – are centrally located as is the well-equipped *Gran Hotel Las Fuentes (206 rooms | Urbanización Las Fuentes | tel. 9 64 41 44 00 | www.fantasia-hoteles.com | Moderate–Expensive, the room prices are based on half or full board, and the hotel is closed in winter)*. The *Playa Tropicana* camping site is a little way outside of town *(Playa Tropicana | Camino de l'Altall |*

PEÑÍSCOLA

tel. 9 64 41 24 63 | www.campingplaya tropicana.com). It is also possible to hire bungalows for 2–5 persons and holiday flats for 2–8 persons in the complex *(Moderate)*; INSIDER TIP good offers in the low season.

with a good restaurant *(106 rooms | Av. Papa Luna 5 | tel. 9 64 47 01 00 | www. parador.es | Moderate–Expensive).* There is also a youth hostel for those with a more restricted holiday budget *(Albergue Juvenil Crist del Mar | Av. de Yecla 29 | tel.*

State of the art: Fishing fleet in the port at Benicarló

On your drive to *Alcossebre* 25km (16mi) to the south-west, you will pass *Alcalá de Xivert.* The village is famous for the Sant Joan Baptista Church with the 68m (223ft)-high bell tower.

BENICARLÓ
(123 F2) (*M G3*)
The small town (pop. 26,000) that starts around 5km (3mi) to the north has a busy port and is mainly attractive as an alternative to spending your holiday in Peñíscola. The best hotel in Benicarló is the *Parador*

9 64 33 64 30 | www.reaj.com | Budget). Of interest in March are the *Fallas (see box p. 53)* with their gigantic constructions, which can be seen all around the town.

SERRA D'IRTA NATURE RESERVE ★
(123 F2–3) (*M G3*)
South of Peñíscola, running parallel to the coast, the hills of the Serra d'Irta – also written Sierra de Hirta – rise up to a height of 573m (1880ft). Many hiking paths traverse the nature reserve *(also*

see Tour 1 under 'Trips & Tours'), and the tourist information office can usually provide you with a helpful general map. Cliffs, pine trees and brush-covered slopes alternate with secluded beaches. The small *Russo* and *Pebret* beaches can only be reached from Peñíscola via a wide bumpy road – with the exception of one small surfaced section – so can only be recommended for sturdy vehicles. The alternative is a lengthy hike. You will pass the ⚡ *Torre Abadum*, a mediaeval Moorish fortified tower; it is no longer permitted to climb up the tower but you will be able to admire the marvellous views of the Mediterranean from all around its base. If you think your car is up to it, you can take the bumpy coastal road from Russo or Pebret to Alcossebre – but be warned, there are deep ruts, dust and gravel! There are also some castle ruins and the former *Sant Antoni* hermitage high up in the mountains.

TORRENOSTRA (123 E3) (*ɰ G3*)

This beach and holiday village (pop. 500) is located around 35km (22mi) southwest of Peñíscola and belongs to the municipality of Torreblanca further inland. The spacious parking area near the large main beach makes this popular for visitors with cars. The *Camping Torrenostra (tel. 9 64 42 50 37)* camping site is open all year long. The *Parc Natural Prat de Cabanes-Torreblanca*, a small nature reserve on the coastal plain mainly made up of marshes and swamps, is located to the south of Torrenostra.

VINARÒS/VINAROZ
(123 F2) (*ɰ G2–3*)

It is worth visiting this small town on the coast (pop. 25,000) 12km (7.5mi) to the north to see the bustling fishing port and the market near the promenade *(mercadillo seminal)* where all kinds of things

are sold on Thursday morning. The most attractive beach is named *Fortí* and the centrally located *Los Arcos Restaurant (closed Wed | Paseo Colón 9 | tel. 9 64 45 56 72 | www.barrestaurantelosarcos. com | Moderate)* serves good tapas, rice and fish dishes, and a reasonably priced daily set menu.
Information office: Plaza de Jovellar | tel. 9 64 45 33 34 | www.turisme.vinaros.es

LOW BUDGET

▶ The city of ● Benicàssim provides bicycles free of charge. At the multi-sport complex, the fleet of two-wheelers waits for guests who want to really get moving *(Pabellón de Deportes | C/. Torre Sant Vicent | Mon–Sat 9am–2pm and 4–9pm, Sun 9am–2pm | tel. 9 64 30 26 62)*. You have to have a passport or other official ID and leave a 50 euro deposit; maximum period: 1 week, minimum age: 18. Further information from the tourist office.

▶ Entrance is free to the *Museu Belles Arts*, Museum of Fine Arts, in ● Castelló de la Plana *(Av. Hermanos Bou 28 | Tue–Sat 10am–8pm, Sun 10am–2pm; in summer, also Mon, 10am–3pm but only until 3pm on Sat)*. See works by Spanish painters such as Gabriel Puig Roda (1865–1919), Vicent Castell Domènech (1871–1934) and Joan Baptista Torcar (1889–1974) who captured scenes of traditional life. In addition, there are halls with sculptures and historical Valencian ceramics, as well as interesting archaeological and folkloric exhibits.

VALENCIA

The **Cathedral** is the main target and the Miguelete bell tower shows the way. Stroll through the Old Town to the Plaza Mayor. The Jardines de Turia begin behind the Torres de Serranos, and the Museum of Fine Arts is only a short walk away on the other side. Well signposted if you arrive by car. Multi-storey car parks: Plaza de la Reina, Pl. Tetuán, P. San Agustín. The city bus Number 8 leaves for the city centre from the bus station at Av. Menéndez Pidal 11.

MAP INSIDE BACK COVER

Valencia (125 D1) *(Ø E6)* – it even sounds beautiful! There is a special atmosphere, a touch of something exotic. The Romans and Moors also felt magnetically drawn to the city and left their mark on the Mediterranean metropolis **(pop. 800,000).**

In 1094, the Spanish national hero El Cid advanced on the city and wrested it from the Muslims for the first time. However, it was not until 1238 that King Jaume I completed the Christian reconquest. Since then, agriculture and trade have helped the *Valencianos* gain prosperity; today it is mainly tourism that keeps the cash reg-

A city full of atmosphere, with beaches and parks, museums and modern architecture – Valencia has something for everyone

isters ringing. The catastrophic flooding of the Turia river in 1957 led to the 'Plan Sur' and the diversion of the river to the south. The drained river bed was turned into a magnificent garden complex and brought verdant colour into the city. That is another plus point in addition to the more than 30 museums in the city. Life is traditional and authentic in the Barri del Carmen, the thousand-year-old city dis-

trict where narrow streets alternate with impressive monuments such as the El Carmen Church. Plenty of energy can also be felt on the square in front of the Town Hall, Plaza del Ayuntamiento.

A dynamic facelift has turned Valencia into one of Spain's most popular destinations for a city trip and the 'City of the Arts and Sciences' has become an international architectural landmark. The splendid

Old Town and many of the promenades were spruced up, the harbour and seafront area changed completely. The Formula One race in (early) summer focuses a great deal of international attention on this charming, vivacious city on the Mediterranean and things also really

Moorish period. The *Puerta de Palau,* one of the three portals of the Cathedral, dates from this early period. The *Puerta de los Hierros* and the multi-figure Gothic *Apostle Portal* on the outside are of particular interest; the *Tribunal de las Aguas* (Water Court) meets in front of it at noon

The spacious exhibition halls of the Institute of Modern Art IVAM

take off during the *Fallas* in March *(see box p. 53).*

Valencia is surrounded by extensive industrial and business parks, as well as orange plantations. Don't be put off by the sober blocks of flats you will see: The city has plenty to offer in the area between the coastline and old quarter! The quality of the water at the beaches is usually extremely good and in the early months of the year there is the aroma of orange blossoms in the air.

on Thursdays *(see box p. 49).* The highlights in the interior are: the *Santo Cáliz Chapel* with the 'Holy Grail', the *Borgia Chapel* with Goya's masterful painting 'San Francisco y el Moribundo Impenitente', the high altar, the arm relic of Saint Vincent Martyr in the *Capilla de la Resurrección,* and the museum with its exhibits of sacred art including paintings by Vicent Macip (1475–1545) one of the most important Renaissance masters in Spain and father of the no less famous painter Juan de Juanes. You should also take the time to climb up the almost 51m (167ft)-high bell tower *El Miguelete* (14th/15th century), a work by Andrés Juliá. The tower is named after Miguel (English: Michael) because the largest bell in it was consecrated on Michaelmas Day. *Cathedral Mon–Sat 10am–6.30pm, Sun 2–6.30pm | Pl. de la Reina*

SIGHTSEEING

CATEDRAL ⭐

The Cathedral shows a heady mix of styles ranging from Gothic to neo-Classicism. The forerunners of the mediaeval house of worship (13th century) were a Roman temple and the main mosque from the

CIUTAT DE LES ARTS I LES CIÈNCIES ★ ●

Dazzling white, curving forms, inlaid work of broken tiles, buildings like monumental sculptures – the modern 'City of the Arts and Sciences', which combines the fascinating architectural concepts of Santiago Calatrava and Félix Candela, offers both culture, and leisure activities. The series of buildings in the complex were all opened in the years between 1998 and 2006 and include the *Palau de les Arts Reina Sofía* (concert hall and opera house), the *Hemisfèric* (Imax cinema) that resembles a gigantic eye, the *Umbracle* (the verdant 'foyer' of the complex), the *Museu de les Ciències Príncipe Felipe* (Museum of Science, *daily 10am–7pm; in summer, 10am–9pm*) and the *Oceanogràfic* (Aquarium, *Sun–Fri 10am–6pm, Sat 10am–8pm, slight variations in early and late summer 10am–7/8pm, mid-July–end of Aug daily 10am–midnight*). Santiago Calatrava's architectural contribution is the *Pont L'Assut d'Or* a steel-and-concrete bridge whose piers that rise up 123m (403ft) are joined by steel cables arranged in the shape of a harp. The audience is drawn into the action taking place on the 9700ft² screen in the *Hemisfèric*; the exhibits in the Science Museum are there to be touched and experimented with. Children will have a lot of fun with the *Espai dels Xiquets* and 'Exploratorium'.

A sculpture measuring 15m (49ft) visualises the genetic fingerprint, a gigantic Foucault's Pendulum demonstrates the rotation of the earth. The highlight of the excellently planned *Oceanogràfic* is the glass tunnel in the 'Oceans' section where sharks and rays float above the heads of the visitors. There are white whales in the 'Arctic' section, penguins in the 'Antarctic' and regular dolphin shows in the *Delfinario*. You will be able to save money if you buy the INSIDER TIP combined ticket for the *Hemisfèric, Science Museum* and *Oceanogràfic. Autovía del Saler | www.cac.es*

INSTITUT VALENCIÀ D'ART MODERN (IVAM) ★

Temporary exhibitions of works by contemporary artists take place in the modern main building. The IVAM has an enormous

---

★ **Catedral**
Awesome building full of art and tradition→ p. 46

★ **Ciutat de les Arts i les Ciències**
Modern architecture that sets new standards → p. 47

★ **Institut Valencià d'Art Modern (IVAM)**
Top address for contemporary art→ p. 47

★ **Jardines del Turia**
The city's 'green lung' developed in the drained bed of the River Turia → p. 48

★ **Lonja de la Seda**
The magnificent Gothic building of the Silk Exchange bears testimony to the prosperity of former times → p. 48

★ **Museu de Belles Arts**
Open Sesame! – Works by Velázquez, El Greco, Goya, Sorolla... → p. 49

★ **Mercat Central/Mercado Central**
One of the most beautiful markets in Spain→ p. 52

★ **L'Albufera**
Nature in its purest form south of the city → p. 54

MARCO POLO HIGHLIGHTS

Magnificent: the columned hall in the Lonja de la Seda

art collection and regularly exchanges works with museums from all over the world. A permanent exhibition is devoted to the oeuvre of the sculptor Julio González (1876–1942). The INSIDER TIP 'Hall of the Great Wall' *Sala de la Muralla*, in which a section of the mediaeval city wall runs between modern columns, is unusual and makes a particularly interesting setting for exhibitions. *Mon/Tue 10am–5pm, Wed–Sun 10am–8pm | Sun free admission | Guillem de Castro 118 | www.ivam.es/en*

JARDINES DEL TURIA ★
After the catastrophic flood in the middle of the 20th century, the River Turia was diverted to the south far away from the city; the dried out riverbed was then used to create new gardens and parks. Today, there are countless palms and orange trees, as well as fountains and even football grounds. The city inhabitants have become very fond of the 7.5km (4.6mi) strip of green that runs through the city all the way to the *Ciutat de les Arts I les Ciències*. Near the Old Town, the Jardines del Turia pass close by the *Torres de Serranos* the massive remains of the mediaeval city walls.

LONJA DE LA SEDA ★ ●
Starting in the late 15th century, merchants went about their business in Valencia's Silk Exchange, which is now one of the Unesco World Heritage Sites. The towering building with its spiral columns combines Gothic with early-Renaissance elements. The Orange Tree Patio adjoins the building. The 'Sea Consulate' next door used to supervise maritime transport. The exchange was once full of tables where the wholesalers and retailers signed their contracts. With a little imagination, the columns can be interpreted as palm trees expanding at the top to support the late-Gothic arches. On Sundays,

the Lonja is the site of a coin and stamp market. *Tue–Sat 10am–2pm and 4.30–8.30pm, Sun 10am–3pm, in summer also Mon 10am–3pm | Pl. del Mercat*

MUSEU ARQUEÒLOGIC DE L'ALMOINA

The splendidly organised Archaeological Museum provides its visitors with fascinating insights into the Roman and Moorish times, as well as other periods. Free admission on weekends. *Tue–Sat 10am–2pm and 4.30–8.30pm, Sun 10am–3pm | Pl. de la Almoina*

MUSEU DE BELLES ARTS ★ ●

The scope of the exhibits in the Museum of Fine Arts ranges from Roman objects and magnificent altar paintings to 20th-century artworks. There are works by all of the famous names in Spanish painting, including Diego de Velázquez, Alonso Cano, Juan Ribalta, Francisco de Goya and Joaquín Sorolla, in addition to an interesting choice of temporary exhibitions. The building dates back to the 17th century when it was an educational establishment for young people who would later play a role in the church. The museum's café is also a nice place to relax. INSIDER TIP *Free admission | Tue–Sun 10am–8pm, in summer Mon/Tue 10am–5pm, Wed–Fri 10am–8pm, Sat/Sun 10am–6pm | C/. San Pio V 9 | museobellasartesvalencia.gva.es*

MUSEU FALLER

Anyone truly interested in the tradition of the *Fallas* festivities in Valencia should visit this museum housed in what used to be a military hospital. You will be able to admire Falla figures that were 'pardoned' at the wish of the people and saved from the flames. *Tue–Sat 10am–2pm and 4.30–8.30pm, Sun 10am–3pm | Pl. Monteolivete 4*

MUSEU NACIONAL DE CERÀMICA

The margrave's *Dos Aguas Palace* forms the impressive frame for this museum that shows much more than just ceramics from various centuries. You will also be able to see halls with precious furniture and porcelain as well as a replica of a Valencian kitchen from the 18th century. The former music and ballroom is elaborately decorated. *Tue–Sat 10am–2pm and 4–8pm, Sun 10am–2pm, Sat afternoon and Sun free admission | Rinconada García Sánchez s/n | mnceramica.mcu.es*

EL PATRIARCA

Valencia's most beautiful Baroque church simply overflows with an abundance of

IT MUST BE TRUE ...

The faithful visit the *Santo Cáliz Chapel* in the Valencia Cathedral to see the legendary chalice used in the Last Supper, which is shown there behind glass (for those who believe it). Women in the last month of pregnancy go to the *Virgen del Coro*, a Gothic painting of the Virgin Mary near the altar. According to tradition, they must make nine circuits of the interior of the Cathedral from this point to guarantee an easy birth and a healthy child. The so-called Water Court *(Tribunal de las Aguas)* meets every Thursday at midday in front of the *Apostle Portal.* Eight ceremoniously robed gentlemen discuss and resolve disputes over water rights; and their decisions are final!

decoration. A very special atmosphere is created with the ● INSIDER TIP Gregorian chants sung by a 20-member choir on Thursday evening at 6.30pm and Tue–Sun during Lauds at 9.30am. The choral tradition dates back to the year 1604. *C/. Nave*

LOW BUDGET

▶ The *Valencia Tourist Card (www. valenciacard.es),* which is available from many hotels and the tourist information offices (at the airport, Pl. de la Reina and other locations), is very helpful for those who want to explore the city in depth. The card provides reductions in selected museums and shops and makes it possible to use public transportation in the A and B tariff zones, as well as the underground to and from the airport, free of charge; the card costs 12 euros for 24, 18 euros for 48 and 22 euros for 72 hours.

▶ Why take an expensive taxi (approx. 20–25 euros) from the airport around 8km (5mi) outside the city when it is just as easy to use the underground *(www.metro valencia.es).* Lines 3 and 5 run to the centre: a single ticket costs 1.90 euros.

▶ The *Puzol* camping site 20 km (12 mi) north-east of Valencia is a less expensive alternative to staying in the metropolis. Mobile homes and bungalows are also available on the site. *Closed mid-Dec–mid-Feb | Playa de Puzol | tel. 9 61 42 15 27 | www.campingpuzol.com.*

PLAZA SANTA CATALINA

Lively inner-city square with the Baroque bell tower of the *Santa Catalina Church.* The cool tiger-nut milk *horchata* is stirred fresh every day in the INSIDER TIP *Horchatería El Siglo.* You can visit the Gothic *Santa Catalina Church* on the adjacent *Plaza Lope de Vega* and buy embroidery and lace on the recently renovated 'Round Square' *Plaza Redonda.*

PLAZA DE LA VIRGEN

Terrace cafés and orange trees create the very special atmosphere of this square at the back of the Cathedral. This was the site of the forum in Roman days. The most important building is the *Basílica Virgen de los Desamparados* where the picture of the 'Holy Virgin of the Defenceless is revered; the main festival for the Virgin Mary is held on the second Sunday in May.

TORRES DE SERRANOS

The defence towers of old Valencia overlook the river bed of the Turia. They were built at the end of the 14th century and are an interesting work from the Gothic period by Pere Balaguer. The towers, that were also used as a prison for the nobility, have stood free since the surrounding city walls were demolished in the 19th century. *Tue–Sat 10am–2pm and 4.30–8.30pm, Sun 10am–3pm, in summer also Mon 10am–3pm*

FOOD & DRINK

There are many typical tapas bars in the Old Town including *El Molinòn (C/. Bolseria 40)* and *El Pilar (C/. Moro Zeit 13).* The vibrant area around the Gran Via Marquès del Turia with restaurants such as *Bodega Pascual (C/. Conde Alta 38)* and *Aquarium (Gran Via Marquès del Turia 57),* is another popular place to enjoy oneself; *all Budget.*

INSIDER TIP ▶
BAMBOO DE COLÓN

Fashionable restaurant that focuses on rice dishes; a little hidden away in the lower section of the Mercat Colón. Very popular with *Valencianos*, modern, unfussy décor, comfortable chairs. The daily set menu served Mon–Fri is especially recommendable. *Closed Sun and Mon evening | C/. Jorge Juan | tel. 9 63 53 03 37 | Moderate*

ness of Mediterranean cuisine. Noble, discreet atmosphere. A wonderful selection of more than 200 wines. *Closed Sun/ Mon | C/. Conde Altea 18 | tel. 9 63 33 53 53 | www.restaurante-riff.com | Expensive*

LA SUCURSAL

Restaurant in the *Institut Valencià d'Art Modern*. The Mediterranean cuisine is just as modern as the ambience. Comprehen-

Functional and modern: Bamboo de Colón Restaurant

PONT DE FUSTA

The inexpensive set menu provides the best reason for trying out this local restaurant. Also serves other simple food; selection of tapas at the bar. *Closed Sun | C/. Santa Amalia 2 | tel. 9 63 69 38 17 | Budget*

RIFF

Chef Bernd Knöller feels that there are only two kinds of food: good and bad. The cook from the Black Forest who has lived in Spain for years really throws himself into everything he does and creates genuine works of art inspired by the fresh-

sive wine list – and, you will be surprised at the many varieties of mineral water. *Closed Sat midday and Sun | Guillem de Castro 118 | tel. 963 74 66 65 | www. restaurantelasucursal.com | Expensive*

EL VENTORRO

Behind its rather unassuming entrance, this traditional restaurant still celebrates dining as a real art. Inviting and cosy; reservations recommended. *Only open Mon–Fri midday and Thu/Fri evening | C/. Bonaire 8 | tel. 963 52 74 01 | www. ventorro.es | Moderate–Expensive*

SHOPPING

The experts have still not made up their minds. Is Barcelona's *Boquería* or the ★● *Mercat Central (Mercado Central)* in Valencia Spain's most beautiful market? The stalls on the 86,000ft² of this Art

Shopping experience: Mercat Central

Nouveau building overflow with sausages, fruit, vegetables, fish and meat. This is where most of the locals prefer to shop – also for cheese, spices, fig marmalade and tomato conserves. Regardless whether you buy anything or not, a visit is always an experience *Mon–Sat 7am–2pm | Pl. del Mercat | www.mercado centralvalencia.es).

There is an elegant shopping area near another historical building, the *Mercat Colón/Mercado Colón* on C/. Jorge Juan. This is where you will find many exclusive shoe shops. All kinds of coloured fabrics are sold in the *Almacenes España (Av. Marqués de Sotelo 3)* and there are several branches of the *El Corte Inglés* department store chain on C/. Pintor Sorolla, Avenida Pio XII, C/. Colón and at other locations. The markets sell all kinds of wares *(mercadillos)*, e.g. on Tue at the *Mercadillo Jerusalén-Pelayo (near the Convento Jerusalén)* and on Wed at the *Mercadillo Mosén Sorell (Pl. Mosén Sorrell)*, and are always full of life.

BEACHES

Valencia has more than 7km (4mi) of beaches. The best section starts north of the port with the connecting *Las Arenas* and *Malvarossa* beaches; they are lined with beautiful promenades.

SPORTS & ACTIVITIES

People jogging, cycling or just going for a walk will find just what they are looking for in the Jardines del Turia and along the beachside promenades. Upon reservation by at least two participants, *Valencia Bikes (Paseo de la Pechina 32 | tel. 963 85 17 40 | www.valenciabikes.com)* organises INSIDER TIP guided cycle tours in English; they also provide the bikes. For those who prefer to be independent, it is also possible to hire bikes for your own individual sightseeing tour. All in all, Valencia has 70km (43mi) of cycle lanes.

ENTERTAINMENT

The hotspots of Valencian nightlife are located in the Old Town quarter *Barri del Carmen* and – especially in summer – behind the beach promenade where you can also chill out in the *Gandhara (Eugenia Viñes 225 | terrazagandhara.com)*. There are DJ sessions, live flamenco and various parties in the INSIDER TIP *Café-Teatro La Claca (C/. San Vicente 3 | www.laclaca. com)*. The INSIDER TIP *Palau de la Música* offers a wide range of performances from classic and jazz to pop *(Paseo de la Alameda 30 | tel. 9 63 37 50 20 | www. palaudevalencia.com)*.

WHERE TO STAY

LAS ARENAS BALNEARIO RESORT
The top house near the marina and directly behind the Las Arenas beach; with its own pool area. The historic predecessor was a 19th-century bathing establishment. The hotel's 'five star Grand Luxe' categorisation is the highest that can be awarded and the rooms are correspondingly spacious and modern. It would be impossible to beat the quality of the breakfast buffet – and the beautiful view towards the seaside promenade with the fountains and lawns is thrown in free of charge. The attached ● *Spa Las Arenas* is a successful symbiosis between tradition and the avant-garde; you can relax at the highest level here every day from 9am to 9pm. *253 rooms | Eugenia Viñes 22–24 | tel. 9 63 12 06 00 | www.h-santos.es | Expensive*

CENTER VALENCIA
Centrally-located youth hostel with good service and free WiFi; the breakfast is also included in the price. Rooms for 4, 6, 8 or 12 persons. *198 beds| C/. Samaniego 8 | tel. 9 63 91 49 15 | www.center-valencia. com | Budget*

CONSUL DEL MAR
Comfortable four-star house with the historical flair of a building from the early 20th century near the *Palau de la Música*. There are no extra charges for using the sauna, small swimming pool and fitness room. *62 rooms | Av. del Puerto 39 | tel. 9 63 62 54 32 | www.krishoteles.com | Expensive*

FIERY GLOW OVER VALENCIA

Valencia throws restraint to the wind every March during the ● *Fallas* – a mega festival that has continued to develop since it started in the 18th century. On 15/16 of the month, colossal effigies and entire ensembles of figures, the so-called *plantà*, are erected everywhere in the city. The gigantic sculptures are real works of art and can be compared with the floats in the large carnival processions in other countries.
The basic materials are usually wood and papier-mâché; the costs sometimes exceed 200,000 euros for a single unit!

The topics range from satirically distorted effigies of politicians to caricatures of the country's football gods, models and other stars. Everybody the people think merits a thrashing gets one. But these artificial figures only have a short lifetime. The, sometimes house-high, sculptures are eventually subjected to flaming scorn in its full sense. On the Night of Fire from 19 to 20 March, they are burnt in the *Cremá* accompanied by gun salutes, fireworks and – to be on the safe side – the fire brigade. *www. fallas.com | www.fallasvalencia.es*

The castle of Cullera beautifully enthroned on a rock above the city

JARDÍN BOTÁNICO
Immerse yourself in luxury and immaculately planned interior design! Intimate, modern, full of light. The room prices vary greatly; the only way to check is online. *16 rooms | C/. Doctor Peset Cervera 6 | tel. 9 63 15 40 12 | www.jardinbotanicohotel valencia.com | Moderate–Expensive*

VENECIA
This functional traditional address in a central location near the Plaza del Ayuntamiento is popular with business people visiting trade fairs. Considerably lower rates in the off-season. *54 rooms | En Llop 5 | tel. 9 63 52 42 67 | www.hotel venecia.com | Moderate*

INFORMATION

Pl. de la Reina 19 | tel. 9 63 15 39 31 | www. turisvalencia.es; other offices at the airport, Renfe railway station and elsewhere

WHERE TO GO

L'ALBUFERA ★
(125 D1–2) (*∅* E6–7)
This nature park with its swamps and rice field starts to the south of the city borders. Its central point is the wide Albufera Lake (Arabic: *albufera* = small sea). Boat tours *(paseos en barca)*, which depart from the eastern side (on the way to El Palmar) enable visitors to admire the varied birdlife, which includes ducks, herons, flamingos and many other species. When the Albufera was much larger, the fishing village of El Palmar was on a small island in the middle of the lake. The boat trip and transfer bus are included in the excursions organised by *Albufera Bus Turístic (starting point on Plaza de la Reina, see: www.valencia busturistic.com for departure times.)* The Albufera Lake is separated from the Mediterranean by a narrow strip of land with pine trees and sand dunes.

CULLERA
(125 D2) (∅ F7)

This pleasant seaside destination (pop. 22,000) for city dwellers in search of relaxation is only around 40km (25mi) south of Valencia; the water park *Aquópolis (see: 'Travel with Kids')* is open during the summer months. The castle, which the Christians conquered from the Moors in 1239, towers over the Old Town. Three-star accommodation in the *Hotel Sicania (116 rooms | Ctra. del Faro s/n | Playa del Racó | tel. 9 61 72 01 43 | www.cullera-hoteles.com | Moderate). www.culleraturismo.com*

SAGUNT/SAGUNTO
(123 D5) (∅ E5)

Sagunt, the small town (pop. 6000) 25km (16mi) north of Valencia has a history going back more than 2000 years, as seen in the *Teatre Romà (Tue–Sat 10am–6pm, in summer to 8pm, Sun 10am–2pm)*. The complex as we see it today has been extensively renovated but in Roman times the theatre could accommodate an audience of 4000. The path up to the castle ☼ from the theatre is lined with cactuses and pine trees. You will also be able to delve deeply into the Roman past in the *Museo Histórico (C/. Castillo 24 | Tue–Sat 11am–6pm, in summer to 8pm, Sun 11am–3pm)*. Sagunt also honours the Fallas tradition in March; the port and beach areas lie a few kilometres away.
Tourist office: Pl. Cronista Chabret | tel. 9 62 65 58 59 | www.sagunt.es

XÀTIVA/JÁTIVA
(124 C3) (∅ E7–8)

Xàtiva/Játiva, surrounded by orange groves and hills, is around 60km (37mi) to the south. There are even two castles on the rocky massif above the pleasant little town; the walls of the *Castillo Mayor* and *Castillo Menor* run picturesquely

across the top of the hills. Mention should also be made of the Fallas tradition in March, the Feria in August and the *Santa María* collegiate church and the memorial to two of the town's most famous sons: the Popes Calisto III (1378–1458) and Alexander VI (1431–1503); both members of the infamous Borgia family. The INSIDER TIP Hotel *Mont Sant* is a stylish place to spend the night *(16 rooms | Subida al Castillo s/n | tel. 962 27 50 81 | www.mont-sant.com | Moderate).*
Tourist office: Alameda Jaume I 50 | tel. 9 62 27 33 46 | www.xativaturismo.com

Grouse also feel at home in the Albufera wetlands

COSTA BLANCA

The Costa Blanca, the 'White Coast', scores with the famous holiday ABC: A for Alacant, B for Benidorm and C for Calp. A number of other towns can also boast perfect beaches and have received the coveted Blue Flag for their cleanliness.

The seasonal differences are just as full of contrasts as the landscapes with their expanses of sand, rocky coasts, bays and mountains in the hinterland. The whirling vivacity in summer brings highlife galore and the inevitable battles for the best places to lay down your towel. A few months later, one has the beaches and promenades almost to oneself and quite a few restaurants and hotels close their doors in winter. However, many of those that stay open make special offers to attract guests who want to escape from the clutches of winter in countries further north. And some people end up making the coast their new home.

ALACANT/ ALICANTE

MAP INSIDE BACK COVER

From the sea, by road or by air – Alacant (125 D6) (*∅ E9–10*) is a hub of plane and car travel, as well as a port

Photo: Beach near Guardamar del Segura

The classic holiday destination: sun, sea and fabulous beaches – and the coast has much more to offer ...

CITY **WHERE TO START?**
Explore the **marina**, then stroll along the Explanada de Espanya to Old Town with the C/. Mayor and Cathedral. Later, you can wander up to the Santa Bárbara Castle. Car parks can be found on the Rambla de Méndez Núñez and at the port.

for cruise ships and yachts. However, the sprawling city (pop. 320,000) is much more than just a way station.

Visitors can experience the lively character of a typical Mediterranean city in the area around the marina and Explanada d'Espanya; the Sant Joan beach area makes an attractive holiday destination. The Romans were the first to enthuse about the special quality of the light

Built by the Moors: Castillo de Santa Bárbara on Monte Benacantil

that today shines over faceless high-rise buildings as well as pleasant promenades and parks such as Monte Tossal and El Palmeral. The highlight of the city's rich heritage is the *Santa Bárbara* Castle.

SIGHTSEEING

OLD TOWN
This compact area is north of the Explanada de Espanya and east of the bustling Rambla de Méndez Núñez with the small pedestrian precinct C/. Mayor (bars, restaurants), the Baroque Town Hall (18th century) and the 17th-century *San Nicolás Cathedral* with its 45m (148ft)-high blue dome. The Old Town is also the site of a mediaeval market *(Mercado Medieval)* in the last week of June and first week in July and people really let their hair down during the city festival celebrating Sant Joan (Saint John) around 20–24 June.

CASTILLO DE SANTA BÁRBARA ★ ● ⋊⋉
The castle complex on the steep Monte Benacantil dominates the scene from an altitude of 166m (545ft) above the city. The origins of the Castillo can be traced back to the early Middle Ages when it was wrested from the Moors by the Spanish troops on Saint Barbara's Day in 1248. The highest section with the oldest remains is called *La Torreta*; part of the castle – with the dungeons and 'Caves of the English' beneath it – is now used for the halls of the new city museum, the *Museo de la Ciudad de Alicante*. There is a lift *(ascensor)* up to the castle from behind the Playa del Postiguet *(in summer daily 10am–10pm; at other times 10am–8pm).* The view is absolutely spectacular!

EXPLANADA DE ESPANYA
Somebody once counted them: the ground of Alacant's showpiece promenade is covered with 2.6 million pieces of marble in black and white and red tones. This is where everybody meets to indulge in their favourite activity of promenading in the shade of the palm trees. The marina is located on the other side of the coastal road.

MUSEO ARQUEOLÓGICO PROVINCIAL

Stroll through the past with its particular focus on prehistoric times up to the Middle Ages. Interesting temporary exhibitions. *Tue–Sa 10–19 (July/Aug 11am–2pm and 6–11pm/midnight), Sun 10am–2pm (July/Aug 11am–2pm) | Pl. del Doctor Gómez Ulla | www.marqalicante.com*

MUSEO DE BELLAS ARTES GRAVINA

Museum of Fine Arts, located in the Baroque *Gravina Palace*. The important regional collection includes paintings and sculptures from the 16th to early 20th century and also shows interesting temporary exhibitions. *Free admission | Tue–Sat 10am–8pm (July/Aug 11am–9pm), Sun 11am–3pm (July/Aug 10am–2pm) | C/. Gravina 13–15 | www.mubag.com*

FOOD & DRINK

LA CASONA ALICANTINA

This traditional restaurant in the pedestrian precinct opened its doors in 1965. Salads, vegetables, meat dishes, daily daily set menu. There are many other restaurants in this price category on the same street. *Daily | C/. Mayor 14 | tel. 9 65 21 24 82 | Budget–Moderate*

NOU MANOLIN

One of the top addresses for gourmets; Mediterranean cuisine using traditional ingredients is served. Reservations recommended! *Daily | C/. Villegas 3 | tel. 9 65 20 03 68 | www.noumanolin.com | Expensive*

SHOPPING

The wide range of goods sold at the various markets including the *Mercado Central (Av. Alfonso X el Sabio | Mon–Sat morning)* and *Mercado Teulada (C/. Teulada | Thu/Fri morning)* makes them attractive places to shop or just watch what is going on.

BEACHES

The best beaches are to the north-east, beginning with the 900m (2950ft) long *Playa del Postiguet* and slightly smaller *Playa de la Albufereta* in the municipal area. The calm water of the *Playa de la Almadraba* makes the beach special and the small bays *(calas)* around *Cabo de las Huertas* have a great deal of charm. Far and away the most popular and longest beach is the *Playa de San Juan (Platja de Sant Joan)* a 3km (almost 2mi) sandy dream.

★ **Castillo de Santa Bárbara**
Alacant's mountain castle opens up beautiful views
→ p. 58

★ **Benidorm Beaches**
Perfect stretches of sand, small bays and the Mediterranean in front of you → p. 63

★ **Fonts de l'Algar/ Fuentes del Algar**
Cascades of water: a heady experience → p. 65

★ **Guadalest**
Magnificent views over the hills and valley → p. 66

★ **Penyal d'Ifac/ Peñón de Ifach**
Calp's local mountain rises up precipitously → p. 68

★ **Palmerar/El Palmeral**
A stroll through the palm grove in Elx is unforgettable
→ p. 74

MARCO POLO HIGHLIGHTS

SPORTS & ACTIVITIES

Boat tours depart from the port for the *Isla de Tabarca (from Kontiki | tel. 9 65 21 63 96 and other organisers)* daily during the summer season, mainly on weekends at other times. There are several golf courses in the vicinity of Alacant including *Alicante Golf (Av. Locutor Vicente Hipólito 37 | Playa de San Juan | tel. 9 65 15 20 43 | www.alicantegolf.org)*, *El Plantío Club de Golf (Ctra. Alacant–Elx, km 3, Partida Bacarot | tel. 9 65 18 91 15 | www.elplantio.com)* and *Club de Golf Alenda (Autovía Alicante–Madrid, km 15, Monforte del Cid | tel. 9 65 62 05 21 | www.alendagolf.com)*.

ENTERTAINMENT

The most popular places to go out and have fun are the vibrant INSIDER TIP marina with its cafés and pubs, the Old Town and the *El Golf* area of the Playa de San Juan. The new construction of the Casino at the port has led to that area becoming less popular. INSIDER TIP The Rockbar *Frontera* is a top address for concerts *(Av. Costa Blanca 140 | Playa de San Juan | tel. 9 65 16 53 35 | www.rockbarfrontera.com)*. You will find a good overview of the month's concerts and other events in the 'Ualà – Revista de Ocio, Cultura y Tendencias' brochure available free of charge from the tourist information offices (in Spanish / *www.revistauala.com)*.

WHERE TO STAY

CASTILLA ALICANTE

Adequate three-star hotel near the Platja de Sant Joan with an outdoor pool in summer, reasonable off-season rates. *155 rooms | Av. Países Escandinavos 7 | tel. 9 65 16 20 33 | www.alicantehotelcastilla.com | Moderate*

GUEST HOUSE

Simple, but cheap: a good address for bargain hunters. Rooms with bathroom, air conditioning and free coffee. Personal

Ideal for a sundowner: evening atmosphere over the port in Alacant

ambience. *9 rooms, 3 studios | C/. Segura 20 | tel. 6 50 71 83 53 | www.guesthouse alicante.com | Budget*

MELIÁ ALICANTE
Complex of several buildings between the marina and Playa del Postiguet. Pool, health club facilities. Occasionally with good special offers online. *545 rooms | Pl. Puerta del Mar 3 | tel. 9 02 14 44 40 | www. solmelia.com | Moderate*

INFORMATION

Rambla de Méndez Núñez 23 (other offices at the bus terminal, Renfe railway station, as well as at Explanada de Espanya 1) | tel. 9 65 20 00 00 | www.alicanteturismo.com

WHERE TO GO

ISLA DE TABARCA
(127 F2) (*⅏ E10*)
Set sail to the south and then continue straight ahead for eleven sea miles to the only inhabited Valencian island (pop. 200) in the Mediterranean. In the second half of the 18th century, Spain's King Carlos III had the former pirate base fortified and sent families from Genoa to settle there. Tabarca's walls are part of the region's cultural heritage; owing to the area's great ecological value, it is also a protected marine reserve and exceedingly popular with divers. On the island – which is only 2km (1.2 mi) long and 400m wide at its broadest point – there is a footpath for visitors who wish to explore. There are not only boat tours from Alacant but also, more frequently, from Santa Pola which is much closer.

SANTA POLA (127 F2) (*⅏ E10*)
Iberians and Romans felt at home here. The sandy beaches are now the main attraction for today's visitors to this small harbour town (pop. 22,000) around 20km (12mi) to the south. Boats depart for the *Isla de Tabarca* throughout the year and there is a *Maritime Museum (Museu del Mar | Tue–Sat 11am–1pm and 4–7pm, (in summer 6.30–9.30pm), Sun 11am–1.30pm)* in the castle. Another attraction is the small aquarium *(Acuario Municipal | Pl. Fernández Ordóñez | in summer daily 11am–1pm and 6–10pm; at other times Tue–Sat 10am–1pm and 4–7pm, Sun 10am–1pm).* Accommodation is available in Hotel *Pola Mar (72 rooms | C/. Astilleros 12 | tel. 9 65 41 32 00 | www. polamar.com | Moderate)*, on the central Platja de Llevant. The most beautiful rooms are on the beach side and the hotel also has a high-class restaurant *(Closed Mon and Sun evenings | Moderate).*

In addition to tourism, the salt-works, whose glittering surfaces and mountains of salt can be seen from afar, are an important economic factor. If you drive on the motorway to the south-west towards Guardamar del Segura/Torrevieja you will pass through the *Salinas de Santa Pola* nature reserve and see miles of salt basins. There is also a salt museum in a historical salt mill *(Museo de la Sal | daily 9am–3pm, Tue/Thu also 4–6pm. Tourist office: Pl. Constitución (Bajos del Ayuntamiento) | tel. 9 66 69 22 76 | www.santa pola.com*

XIXONA/JIJONA (125 D5) (*⅏ E9*)
The small town to the north with a Moorish past (pop. 8000) 25km (16mi) to the north is a household word throughout Spain on account of its production of marzipan and traditional almond-and-honey, nougat-like sweets *(turrones)*. You can visit the *Museo del Turrón (Mon–Fri 10am– 1.30pm and 4–7.30pm, (July–Dec 10am– 7.30pm), Sat 10am–1pm and 4–7pm, Sun 10am–1pm and 5–7pm | Ciudad del Turrón | www.museodelturron.com).*

BENIDORM

(125 E5) *(⑪ F9)* **Today, 'Manhattan on the Mediterranean' (pop. 74,000) has become a synonym for uninhibited leisure and holiday fun. People who come in the high season know exactly what they want: their focus is probably not as much on pure relaxation as unbridled fun.**

The statistics list more than 1000 bars, cafeterias, restaurants and discos. In addition there are tens of thousands of beds in the hotels, guest houses and blocks of holiday flats – and not everybody wakes up where he or she expected at the end of a long, turbulent night …

Once upon a time, the sea rolled onto deserted beaches in Benidorm. At the end of the 1950s, only 3000 people lived here and most of them earned their livelihood from fishing or farming. Shortly afterwards, mass tourism started and it has left an indelible mark on Benidorm. However, things calm down in the off-season.

board an unmanned ship drifting off the coast and that it even survived a fire.

FOOD & DRINK

There are many tapas bars on C/. de Santo Domingo and the neighbouring streets in the pedestrian precinct, as well as on C/. Martínez Oriola.

CLUB NÁUTICO

A pleasant place to dine near the marina; you can see part of Benidorm's skyline through the large windows. Freshly-caught fish are sold by weight (the menu lists the price per 100g). *Daily | Paseo Colón, Puerto | tel. 9 65 85 54 25 | Moderate–Expensive*

ULÍA

Sophisticated dining on the beach promenade behind the Playa de Poniente. Squid, rice with lobster, seafood paella, paella with rabbit. *Closed Sun evening and Mon | Av. Vicente Llorca Alós | near the corner of C/. Vigo | tel. 9 65 85 68 28 | Moderate*

SIGHTSEEING

OLD TOWN

Benidorm's historical origins – the settlement dates from the 14th century – are restricted to a relatively small area between the port and Playa de Levante. The name of a square is the only thing that recalls the late mediaeval castle from which the local population defended themselves against pirates from North Africa: *Plaza del Castell.* The ☆ promenades and platforms with views of the two main beaches are nice though. The most important building is the *Sant Jaume* Church built in the 18th century on Plaza Sant Jaume. A statue of the patron saint the Virgen del Sufragio is honoured in the church: it is said that the wondrous sculpture of the Virgin Mary was discovered in 1740 on

SHOPPING

The lively hustle and bustle begins behind the Playa de Levante on *Avenida Martínez Alejos* and continues on to the *Plaça de la Creu*. The vitality that can be felt there is what makes the shopping areas interesting. Of course, those who buy in the 'nothing over 3 euros' shops get quality to match the price. In the direction of the Playa de Poniente, the pedestrian precinct ends near the Parque de Elche with its grove of palm trees.

BEACHES

⭐ The uncontested queens among the many beaches are the ● *Platja de Llevant/Playa de Levant* (East Beach; 2.1km (1.3mi) long) and ● *Platja de Ponent/Playa de Poniente* (West Beach; 3.1km (1.9mi) long). The two are separated by a promontory with the Old Town behind it. The port adjoins the Platja de Ponent with the tiny, only 120m (390ft)-long', *Mal Pas Beach*

near it. Two small bays behind the Platja de Levant, the *Cala Almadrava* and *Cala del Ti Ximo*, display their rugged charm. Another rocky promontory, where the Iberians once lived, separates the Platja de Ponent from the *Cala de Finestrat*, a lovely sandy bay, to the south-west.

SPORTS & ACTIVITIES

Excursion boats set sail regularly from the port in Benidorm; some of them have glass bottoms so that the passengers can see the submarine world (*www.excursiones maritimasbenidorm.com*). The *Isla de Benidorm, Altea* and *Calp* are just three of the many destinations. There are also fishing trips and night cruises. Hiking trails make it possible to explore the bordering *Sierra Helada*; information from the tourist office. Joggers will find plenty of room on the beaches and promenades – in the off-season. Jeep safaris, paintball, bicycle hire from *Marco Polo Expediciones (Av. Europa 5 | tel. 965*

Manhattan on the Mediterranean: Benidorm's skyline

86 33 99 | www.marcopolo-exp.es). The *Rancho Sierra Helada (Carretera Diputación s/n | mobile phone 610 91 74 46)* organises horseback rides. There are also several fun parks, including *Mundomar, Terra Mítica* and *Terra Natura (see: 'Travel with Kids')*, as well as a water park *Aqualandia (www.aqualandia.net)*, in or near Benidorm.

ENTERTAINMENT

There is a whole row of discotheques along the north-eastern road out of town towards Altea *(Av. Comunitat Valenciana)* including *KU, Racha Rock* and *Penelope*, while the lavish revue programme with dinner in the *Benidorm Palace (Av. Severo Ochoa 13 | tel. 9 65 85 16 60 | www.benidorm-palace.com)* attracts a completely different audience. Concerts ranging from classical music to blues are held in the *Aula de Cultura Cam (C/. Alameda 17 | tel. 9 65 85 07 05)*.

WHERE TO STAY

GRAN HOTEL BALI ☆☆

Two-towered giant that sets new standards in the already impressive skyline of Benidorm. The higher building soars 186m (610ft) into the sky. A supplement is charged for rooms on the 30th–41st floors. Pools, restaurants, fitness centre. Room prices are based on half board. *776 rooms | C/. Luis Prendes 4 | tel. 9 02 14 15 14 | www.granhotelbali.com | Moderate–Expensive*

LA CALA

Charming hotel that is unfortunately closed from early November to the beginning of March. Acceptable quality, decent ensuite rooms but without sea views; there are sometimes attractive offers on the homepage. *40 rooms | Av. Marina Baixa 10 | Cala de Finestrat | tel. 9 65 85 46 62 | www.hotel-lacala.com | Moderate*

INSIDER TIP ▶ **EL PALMERAL**
Pleasant house one street back from the seaside behind the Playa de Poniente. Some rooms have views of the Mediterranean and there is also a tiny outdoor swimming pool. Good service and food. *Closed Nov–March | 60 rooms | C/. Altea 2 | Playa de Poniente | tel. 9 65 85 01 76 | www. hotelpalmeral.com | Budget–Moderate*

INFORMATION

Av. Martínez Alejos 16 | tel. 9 65 85 13 11 | turismo.benidorm.org

WHERE TO GO

ALCOI/ALCOY (125 D4) *(⍉ E8)*

Surrounded by mountains and with two nature parks, *Serra Mariola* and *Carrascar de la Font Roja*, only a stone's throw away, this small town (pop. 62,000), 50km (31mi) to the north-west is a popular inland destination. You should take the **INSIDER TIP** beautiful mountain route via Guadalest, Confrides and Benillloba on your way there or back. Alcoi is visited by streams of visitors every year in April or May for the *Moros y Cristianos* festivities: these celebrate the battles between the Moors and Christians in the Middle Ages. Around 5000 people take part in the processions. Alcoi's historical district, some of the Art Nouveau buildings, the metal structure of the *Viaducto de Canalejas* erected at the beginning of the 20th century and the *Archaeological Museum (Museu Arqueològic | Placeta del Carbó | Mon 9am–2pm, Tue–Fri 9am–2pm and 4–7pm, Sat/Sun 10.30am–1.30pm)* in the Old Town Hall (16th century) are well worth a visit. You will find tapas bars on streets such as C/. Pintor Casanova and

Beautiful Art Nouveau facades in Alcoi

squares like the Pl. Pintor Gisbert, as well as decent accommodation in the *Hostal Savoy (29 rooms | C/. Casablanca 9 | tel. 9 65 54 72 72 | www.hostalsavoy.com | Budget).*
Tourist information: Pl. d'Espanya 14 | tel. 9 65 53 71 55 | www.alcoiturisme.com

ALTEA (125 E5) (*M F9*)

This small town (pop. 21,000) is about 10km (6mi) to the north-east; it is divided between the Old Town on the hill and the newer coastal district. There is plenty of activity near the sea around the marina and fishing port and along the Passeig del Mediterrani; the *San Miguel Restaurant (Sant Pere 7 | tel. 9 65 84 04 00 | closed Sat and Sun evening and Tue | Budget–Moderate)* has served traditional fish and rice dishes for decades. On the other side of the through road, the scene immediately changes to that of simple village life. Laundry flutters above the narrow lanes and the balconies overflow with flowers.

A long ascent leads up to the church square, several bars and the entrance to the ⚜️ *Mirador Cronistes d'Espanya* with a panoramic view as far as the skyline of Benidorm.

FONTS DEL'ALGAR/FUENTES DEL ALGAR ★ ☺ (125 E5) (*M F9*)

Thundering waterfalls, crystal-clear water behind the dam, little bridges across the river – it is not without reason that the *Algar Springs (Aug daily 10am–7.30pm, July/Sep 10am–7pm, varying opening hours in other months 10am–5/5.30/6pm)* 15km (9mi) to the north near Callosa d'en Sarrià promotes itself as a small natural paradise. You can usually get a general plan at the ticket booth but even without one you will not get lost on the network of paths leading upstream. It is also possible to go swimming in some places – at your own risk. The area has been carefully adapted to tourism but there are people near the entrance who try to take

Once besieged by Christian soldiers; today, by tourists: Guadalest

advantage of the limited parking space and overcharge. There are several restaurants; unfortunately, most of them are more interested in quantity than quality. On the other hand, we can recommend that you buy INSIDER TIP loquat products (juice, fruit in syrup, honey, schnapps) with the protected designation of origin from Callosa d'en Sarrià. There is an interesting cactus garden about 1000m above Fonts de l'Algar. Further information on Fonts de l'Algar under: *tel. 9 65 88 01 53 | www.lasfuentesdelalgar.com*

GUADALEST ★ ⋇
(125 E4–5) (*Ø F8–9*)
Welcome to this dream village of stone! When one considers that only about 200 people live here, Guadalest is in fact subject to one of the largest onslaughts in Spain, receiving around 2 million visitors every year. There is rarely a lull in activities

in Guadalest. After you get past the strip of souvenir shops, you enter a tunnel leading to the historical centre that is overlooked by a castle. The views of the surrounding countryside are fantastic: the rugged mountains above and the glittering water of the Guadalest reservoir below in the valley. Museum culture also plays a role here, including the folkloric *Casa Orduña* and 'Magic Garden' with sculptures. The *Torture Museum (Museo de Tortura | daily 11am–7pm, later in the evening in summer, depending on number of visitors)* describes its function to be a 'testimony against brutality', and exhibits more than 70 instruments and apparatuses of torture – from gallows and grills to the rack and the guillotine. The INSIDER TIP *Museo de Microminiaturas* and *Museo de Microgigante (both Tue–Sun 10am–6pm, to 8pm in summer)* where visitors can admire miniature paintings –

such as Goya's 'Naked Maya' on a fly's wing – by the artist Manual Ussá is something of a curiosity. Guadalest is also known as *El Castell de Guadalest* and lies 20km (12mi) north-west of Benidorm.
Information: Oficina de Turismo | Av. de Alicante s/n | tel. 9 65 88 52 98 | www. guadalest.es

TERRA MITICA (125 E5) (*ØØ F9*)

The curtain rises on 'The Mummy's Curse', 'The Labyrinth of the Minotaur' and 'The Cataracts of the Nile'. It's show and fun time in this gigantic amusement park behind Benidorm. Organised entertainment everywhere; a choice between wild and more peaceful rides for all age groups. The old cultures of the Mediterranean region form the leitmotif: from the Egyptians and Greeks to the Romans and Iberians. *Mid-April–beginning of Dec, changing opening times, outside the main season sometimes only Thu–Sun 10am–8pm, mid-July–beginning of Aug daily 10am–2am | one-day ticket 35 euros, children (5–10 years) 26.50 euros, reduced evening ticket 22 euros, children 18 euros | Partida del Moralet s/n | well-signposted approach | tel. 9 02 02 02 20 | www.terra miticapark.com*

LA VILA JOIOSA/VILLAJOYOSA (125 D–E5) (*ØØ F9*)

Colourful house facades in orange, blue and red are the silent symbols of this small harbour town (pop. 30,000) 10km (6mi) to the south-west on the coast. The former fishing village is a seaside alternative to Benidorm but there is no comparison with the night life in the bigger town. The small Old Town district with the *Assumpció Church* is charming; the *Moros y Cristianos* festival is celebrated here at the end of July.
Tourist office: C/. Colón 40 | tel. 9 66 85 13 71 | www.villajoyosa.com

CALP/CALPE

(125 E5) (*ØØ F9*) **A town, a rocky massif, an eye-catcher – the soaring flanks of the Penyal d'Ifac/Peñón de Ifach, one of the symbols of the Mediterranean coast.**

Early Phoenician mariners admired the 332m (1089ft)-high limestone rock that rises up behind Calp and called it the 'Rock of the North'. The small seaside town and port (pop. 30,000) that stretches along the coast at its base was once a fishing village. In 1238, the Christians took Calp back from the Moors and soon afterwards started exploiting the salt in the area. In 1744, in a legendary attack, they drove back 800 pirates heading towards the shore on five large ships. In recent years, many people from other parts of Europe have settled in the area and a blanket of houses now reaches far up into the hills. The salt works are of historical importance and significant modern developments are seen in the work of Spanish architect Ricardo Bofill: *La Muralla Roja, El Anfitteatro* and *Xanadú*.

SIGHTSEEING

OLD TOWN

Calp's Old Town is mainly visible in the area around the Plaza de la Vila, in the remains of the city wall, the Gothic Mudéjar-style church (15th century) and the *Collectors' Museum (Museo del Coleccionismo | in summer daily 10.30am–1.30pm and 6–10pm, at other times Tue–Sun 10.30am–1.30pm and 5–8pm).*

HARBOUR

The lively sport and fishing harbour brings together elegant yachts and local fishermen mending their nets. Many restaurants focus on seafood: the fish auction takes place at around 4 or 5pm from Monday to Saturday.

CALP/CALPE

PENYAL D'IFAC/
PEÑÓN DE IFACH ★ ☆

Calp's gigantic rock, a designated *Parc Natural*, is the habitat of numerous seabirds and home to hundreds of species of plants. The *Passeig Ecològic Principe de Asturias*, a well-maintained path, curves its way around the west and south precipices. Overshadowed by the massive Peñón, it

varieties of paella. Large terrace. *Closed Tue and in Nov | Explanada del Puerto | tel. 9 65 83 85 93 | Budget–Moderate*

LOS DOS CAÑONES

This simple restaurant with a lovely terrace is located directly opposite the city wall and serves lamb chops, entrecôte, as well as vegetarian paella. *Closed Oct–April*

Mountain hikers are offered spectacular views from Penyal d'Ifac

continues past the stony *El Racó Bay*, past lanterns, palm trees and mimosas and opens up wonderful views of the coast and mountains. The ascent of the Peñón is rewarded with magnificent panoramas; however, the climb is extremely strenuous and only recommended for experienced mountain hikers (approx. 2–2.5 hours). On the way, the path also passes a tunnel that was cut into the rock in 1918.

and Sun evening | C/. Trinquet 2 | tel. 9 65 83 74 92 | Budget–Moderate

SHOPPING

On Wednesdays, the weekly flea market takes place opposite the *Pabellón Municipal de Deportes* and, on Saturdays, there is a regular street market in the area of *Avenida Puerto Santa María/Avenida del Norte*.

FOOD & DRINK

LAS BARCAS

Enjoy the atmosphere of the port either with the daily set menu or one of the many

BEACHES

Calp's beaches are located on both sides of the Peñón de Ifach. To the west – starting behind the port – these include the small *Playa Cantal-Roig* (the Romans used to salt their fish near the Baños de la Reina), the *Cala Morelló* and the 1200m-long strip of sand that makes up the *Playa de Levante* (also: *Playa La Fossa*).

SPORTS & ACTIVITIES

In summer, a variety of boat tours, both along the coast and to Altea and Benidorm, depart from the port. Bicycles can be hired from *Sol y Bike (C/. Blasco Ibañez 10-A | tel. 6 76 86 74 45 | www.solybike.com).* The *Centro de Deportes Náuticos Las Antí podas (Ctra. Calpe–Moraira, km 2 | tel. 9 65 83 83 10 | www.lasantipodas.com)* organises many water-sports activities such as sailing, sea kayaking and windsurfing.

ENTERTAINMENT

The bars and pubs such as the *Álamo (C/. La Santamaría 5)*, *Delfín (C/. Delfín)* and *Hollywood (C/. La Pinta)* are popular meeting places. The *Discoteca Blue Bay* is in C/. Ponent. Concerts and other events are held in the *Casa de Cultura Jaume Pastor i Fluixà (Av. Masnou 1 | tel. 9 65 83 91 23 | www.cultura.calpe.es).*

WHERE TO STAY

APARTHOTEL EUROPA
Not very attractive from the outside but this block of flats boasts a prime location directly behind the beach promenade. Holiday flats for up to five people with balconies. *144 units | Av. Europa 21 | tel. 9 65 83 54 95 | www.aparthoteleuropa.es | Moderate*

INSIDER TIP **GRAN SOL**
This small, informal hotel with a swimming pool is located a little way out of town. The room prices include breakfast. Reasonable rates in the off-season; good value

for money. *12 rooms | Urbanización Gran Sol 6 B | tel. 9 65 83 62 82 | www.hotel gransolcalpe.com | Budget*

INFORMATION

Pl. del Mosquit s/n | tel. 9 65 83 85 32 | www.calpe.es

WHERE TO GO

MORAIRA (125 F4) (*M* G8)
A densely settled stretch of coast with many bays, and coastline shared by villas and pine trees, separates Calp from Moraira – the municipality is called *Teulada-Moraira* (pop. 12,000) – around 15km (9mi) to the north-west. The bulky round tower of the *castle* (18th century) between the *Platja de l'Ampolla* and port presents a distinctive landmark. There are vineyards in the environs. *Tourist office: Ctra. Moraira–Teulada 51 | tel. 9 65 74 51 68 | www.teulada-moraira.es*

DÉNIA

(125 F4) (*M* F8) The gateway to the Costa Blanca and springboard (ferry port) to the Balearic Islands, Dénia (pop. 47,000) gives guests a warm, cosmopolitan welcome and has retained its maritime character.

The area around Dénia is densely settled, but fortunately there are fewer high-rise buildings than on many other sections of the coast. The city was called Dianium in Roman times, the Moors named it Daniya until it was conquered by the Spanish Christians. The areas you should visit are clearly defined; the broad harbour front, the castle on the hill and the sandy beaches. There is also a lively town centre around *C/. del Cop* and *C/. Marqués de Campo*.

DÉNIA

Inland, orange groves spread across the landscape as far as the eye can see, while the panoramic view to the south-east stops at the precipitous *Montgó Massif* with the cliffs at its feet. Dénia has built up a good culinary reputation for its *gambas*. It is always fun to watch the fishing boats return to port – between 3.30 and 6pm on weekdays.

SIGHTSEEING

CASTLE ☆

The path up to the walls and castle starts behind the arcaded front of the town hall and you will soon see a Muslim archway. The *Torre Islámica*, a well-preserved tower, which can be reached along a path leading through a lovely pine grove, is another indication of Moorish presence. From here, you will have your first good view of the Montgó Massif. You might be out of breath when you finally reach the top plateau with the *Palau del Gobernador* and *Museu Arqueològic*, the entrance fee includes admission to the small archaeological museum. Concerts are occasionally held in the castle in summer and there is a very special atmosphere on the INSIDER TIP night visits in July and August. *July/Aug daily 10am–1.30pm and 5pm–0.30am (except when concerts are held), Jun/Sep 10am–1.30pm and 4–7.30/8pm, changes almost monthly at other times 10am–1/1.30pm and 3/3.30/4–5/6/7pm*

MUSEU DELS JOGUETS

Toy museum with doll's houses and cars from times gone by. Entrance free, austere ambience. *Daily 10am–1pm, 4–8pm (In summer 5–9pm) | C/. Calderón s/n*

FOOD & DRINK

CHIMICHURRI

Popular meeting place at the marina with cheese or ham dishes as a starter. Good selection of salads and, above all, grilled

The castle has watched over the port in Dénia for centuries

meat. *Daily | Puerto Deportivo | tel. 966 42 55 31 | www.chimichurridenia.com | Moderate–Expensive*

MENA

With a large terrace overlooking the coast near Platja Arenetes, Mena's selection ranges from entrecôte to sea bass and platters of grilled fish. There are also special meals for children. *Closed Sun evening and, depending on the season, Wed | Final de las Rotas | tel. 9 65 78 09 43 | Moderate*

SHOPPING

The ☺ weekly market, where you can also buy organically grown products, is held in the hall on *C/. Magallanes (Mon–Sat 7am–2pm)*; sometimes there are also a few stands outside. A *mercadillo* (market for all kinds of goods) is held on the *Explanada Torrequemada* on Monday morning as is a *rastro de antigüedades* (flea and antiques market) on Friday morning. In summer, there is a *mercadillo* on the *Explanada Cervantes (until around midnight)*. During the orange season (Oct–April) you can buy fruit by the bucket in many places, e.g. on the road to Gandia.

BEACHES

● Dénia has around 20km (12mi) of coastline separated into the northern (*Área Les Marines*) and southern beaches (*Playas de las Rotas*) by the port. While the 'northern beaches' score top marks for their wide expanses of yellow sand, the 'southern beaches' offer a string of smaller, rather stony, coves. The only exception is the sandy *Marineta Cassiana* near the port.

SPORTS & ACTIVITIES

It is possible to **INSIDER TIP** walk for miles along the seashore, from the city centre, past the *Platja Marineta Cassiana* and *Platja El Trampoli* and as far as the *Punta Negra;* the route includes surfaced promenade, dirt paths and small side roads, of which are well suited for jogging. Excursion boats depart regularly from the port; e.g. *Mundo Marino (www.mundomarino.es)*. A popular hiking destination, the *Parc Natural Montgó,* is only a short distance away (the tourist office can provide a pamphlet with information on the park). You can choose between several hiking trails starting from the entrance at *Camí del Pou de la Montaña;* these include one to the *Cova de l'Aigua* (1.6km/1mi), one to the *Racó del Bou* (2.6km/1.6mi) and another up to the 753m (2470ft)-high peak (*Creueta*, 8.5km/5.3mi).

ENTERTAINMENT

The trendiest place to go out at night is on the south side of the marina (*Escullera Sud*). There you can enjoy the flair of the port with its numerous pubs, bars and restaurants; the area around C/. La Mar is also quite popular. There are several discos in summer including *Magma (Carretera Las Marinas | Urbanización Les Fonts)*.

WHERE TO STAY

BUENAVISTA

A country hotel just outside Dénia, this 19th-century house is surrounded by 4 acres of land. This tranquillity can be enjoyed next to the pool; all-round comfort. *17 rooms | Partida del Tossalet 82 | tel. 9 65 78 79 95 | www.buenavistadenia.com | Expensive*

CRISTINA

In the Old Town and perfect if you have to watch your budget. Simple and functional, rooms with bathroom; free Wi-Fi. *20 rooms | Av. del Cid 5 | tel. 9 66 42 31 58 | www.hostal-cristina.com | Budget*

DÉNIA

LES ROTES

Modern design throughout, pleasant pool area and only a few hundred metres walk from the seaside promenade. A supplement is charged for rooms with a sea view and terrace. Drivers will find the hotel's car park convenient and there is a bus stop on the road with connections to the city centre 4km (2.5mi) away. Four stars, with restaurant. Prices include breakfast. *33 rooms | Ctra. Barranc del Monyo 85 | Les Rotes | tel. 9 65 78 03 23 | www.hotel lesrotes.com | Expensive*

INFORMATION

C/. Manuel Lattur 1 | tel. 9 66 42 23 67 | www.denia.net

WHERE TO GO

COVA DE LES CALAVERES/CUEVA DE LAS CALAVERAS (125 E4) (*∅ F8*)

The grotto with the martial-sounding name of 'Skull Cave' is also known as *Cova de Benidoleig* and once provided shelter for prehistoric people. 'Skull Cave' refers to the human bones from the Islamic period that were found there; it is assumed that some Moors became trapped inside the cave while they were looking for water. The story about a Moorish prince who supposedly tried to protect himself and the 150 people in his harem from El Cid in the cave can probably be relegated to the realm of legend. *14km (9mi) south-west of Dénia | daily, in summer 9am–8pm, at other times 9am–6pm| www.cuevadelas calaveras.com*

GANDIA/GANDÍA (125 E3) (*∅ F8*)

Located about 30km (19 miles) to the north-west of Dénia, the city (pop. 76,000) is divided into an inland and coastal section. The broad beach, which stretches for miles, and its spacious promenade start near the Nautic Club. There, you will also find the *tourist information office (Passeig Maritim Neptú 45 | tel. 9 62 84 24 07 | www.gandia.org)*. Seafood and the wonderful view from the terrace are the highlights of the Restaurante *Ripoll (daily | Passeig Maritim Neptú, Dique Norte | tel. 9 62 84 67 43 | Moderate)*. The *Palau dels Borja*, the palace of the counts of the infamous Borgia family, is located in the centre of Gandia *(C/. Duc Alfons el Vell 1 | tours Tue–Sat 10am–1pm and 4–6.30pm, in summer to 7pm and Sun 10am–1pm)*.

XÀBIA/JÁVEA, CAP DE LA NAO (125 F4) (*∅ G8*)

Xàbia (Spanish: Jávea; pop. 30,000), 10km (6mi) to the south-east, extends along the coast and can boast some beautiful beaches; at the top of the list is *Platja de l'Arenal* where visitors will find plenty of places to stop for refreshments. The *Parador*, a four-star hotel surrounded by a grove of palm trees, provides exquisite accommodation at the other end of the promenade *(70 rooms | Av. del Mediterráneo 7 | tel. 9 65 79 02 00 | www. parador.es | Expensive)*.

The harbour spreads out below Cap Sant Antoni, and a second promontory juts out into the sea south-east of Xàbia: *Cap del Nao* (also written as *Nau*). The signposted road to the cape leads through a widespread villa area from where some roads turn off to the individual bays *(Portitxol, Ambolo* nudist zone). A lighthouse rises up above the cape, swimmers listen to the cries of the seagulls, there is the aroma of pine and lavender in the air and wonderful panoramic views of the rocky coast.

Tourist office in the centre of Xàbia: Pl. Església 4 | tel. 9 65 79 43 56 | www.xabia. org

ELX/ELCHE

MAP INSIDE BACK COVER

Palms, palms – nothing but palms! There are almost as many palm trees as residents in Elx (pop. 220,000) (124 C6) (*ΩΩ D10*), around 15km (9mi) from the coast. The 200,000 magnificent specimens are protected by law.

was created 2500 years ago when the city was called Heliké. Besides the architecture that bears witness to the time of the Moors, such as the castle *Alcàsser de la Senyoria* (with the Archaeological Museum) and the chunky *La Calaforra* tower, modern architecture has also started occupying the cityscape. Shoe manufacturing is an important source of income.

Secluded rocky cove at Cap de la Nao near Xàbia

Palmerar/El Palmeral, the grove of palm trees that was laid out under Moorish rule is considered the largest of its kind in Europe and is on Unesco's World Heritage List. During their occupation, the Moors not only created verdant gardens but, as experts in oasis cultivation, they were able to develop agriculture by using sophisticated irrigation methods. The famous statue of the 'Lady from Elche'

SIGHTSEEING

BANYS ÀRABS

Dip into the remains of an underground Moorish bathing complex from the 12th century where people used to meet not only to wash but to socialise. *Tue–Sat 10am–1.30pm and 4.30–8pm, Sun 10.30am–1.30pm | Passeig de les Eres de Santa Llúcia 13*

BASILICA DE SANTA MARÍA

The basilica from the 17th/18th century with its high, blue-tiled, dome and dazzling gold main altar is the venue of the *Misteri d'Elx* in August. Visitors who climb to the top of the 37m (121ft)-high tower are rewarded with a magnificent view *(daily 11am–6pm, in summer to 7pm)*.

MUSEU D'ART CONTEMPORANI

Museum for contemporary art showing works by Spanish avant-garde artists including Juana Francés and *Grup d'Elx*. *Tue–Sat 9.30am–1.30pm, 5–8pm, Sun 10.30am–1.30pm | Pl. Major del Raval 1*

MUSEU MUNICIPAL DE LA FESTA

Exhibition on the mystery play of Elx *(see box)*; there are audiovisual presentations several times a day. *Tue–Sat 10am–1.30pm and 4.30–8pm, Sun 10am–1pm | C/. Major de la Vila 25*

MUSEU DEL PALMERAR

Documentation centre with information on the palm grove; the museum is in a 19th-century house near the Huerto del Cura. *Tue–Sat 10am–1.30pm, 4.30–8pm, Sun 10.30am–1.30pm | Porta de la Morera 12*

PALMERAR/EL PALMERAL ★

This name refers to all the magnificent date palms in Elx, which are to be found in many areas and garden complexes in the town. The most popular of the palm parks begins immediately behind the remains of the city walls and Moorish castle *Alcàsser del al Senyoria.* The *Parc Municipal* is exceedingly well laid out with countless paths, benches, groups of plants, flower beds, drinking fountains, children's playground facilities and a bandstand. The information office and a visitor centre *(Centre de Visitants | Mon–Sat 10am–7pm, Sun 10am–2pm)* are located on the edge of this city park.

But, the ● *Huerto del Cura* is the palm grove to end all palm groves! You can wander among palm trees, ponds, fountains and Mediterranean and exotic plants in one of the most beautiful oases in Spain – a complex straight out of a picture-book that is classified as a 'National Artistic Garden' and is definitely worth the money charged for admission! INSIDER TIP You can also stock up on dates in the shop. *Porta de la Morera 49 | Nov–Feb daily 10am–5.30/6pm, at other times 7pm, in summer to 9pm | www.huertodelcura.com*

DRAMA IN THE CHURCH

Every year on 14 and 15 August, a liturgical drama accompanied by music is on the programme in Elx's Santa María Basilica: the mystery play *(Misteri d'Elx)* that has been performed since the late Middle Ages consists of two parts and has now become a lavishly staged public spectacle. The play deals with the death, ascension and coronation of the Holy Virgin and Mother of God Mary. Sophisticated equipment even makes it possible for the performers to hover through the space of the church. Tickets are also sold for the dress rehearsals on 11, 12 and 13 August. *Information on tickets, seats, prices and starting times are available from the tourist office in Elx or online under: www. misteridelx.com.*

Palms, cactuses, ponds: the enchanting Huerto del Cura park

PARC ARQUEOLÒGIC I MUSEU DE L'ALCUDIA

Archaeological park with traces of the settlements that preceded today's Elx, located a short distance out of town. *Tue–Sat 10am–8pm, at other times Tue–Sat 10am–5pm, Sun always 10am–3pm | Ctra. de Dolores | km 2*

FOOD & DRINK

MESÓN EL GRANAINO

Exquisite traditional cooking with an Andalusian touch. The restaurant also serves simple dishes such as potatoes prepared with spicy paprika *(pimentón)* from Vera. *Closed Sun | José María Buch 40 | tel. 9 66 66 40 80 | Budget–Moderate*

EL PERNIL

Tasty, well-balanced Mediterranean cuisine starring (naturally) fish and seafood. There is also a fairly inexpensive daily daily set menu. *Closed Sun in summer |*
Juan Ramón Jiménez 4 | tel. 9 66 61 33 03 | Moderate

WHERE TO STAY

HUERTO DEL CURA

Well-kept, four-star house surrounded by magnificent gardens and near a beautiful grove of palm trees. *81 rooms | Porta de la Morera 14 | tel. 9 66 61 20 50 | www.hotelhuertodelcura.com | Moderate–Expensive*

MILENIO

Elegant, appealing hotel nestled among the palm trees. With outdoor pool and restaurant. *72 rooms | Prolongación de Curtidores s/n | tel. 9 66 61 20 33 | www.hotelmilenio.com | Moderate*

INFORMATION

Parc Municipal | tel. 9 66 65 81 95 | turismedelx.com

WHERE TO GO

GUARDAMAR DEL SEGURA
(127 E3) (*m̨ D10*)

Situated at the mouth of the Riu Segura, this small town (pop. 17,000; 20km/12mi south-east of Elx) encircled by belts of pine and eucalyptus trees, beaches and dunes, is a nature-lover's paradise. The *Parque Alfonso XII* is a splendid complex that starts directly behind the *Babilònia* and *Vivers* beaches and stretches as far as the fishing port *Marina de las Dunas*. The numerous paths in the park invite visitors to take lengthy strolls through the greenery and admire the remains from Phoenician times (*Yacimiento Fenicio,* 8th century BC) and the Moorish period (*Rabita Califal,* 10th century). The Old Town, founded in the 13th century and severely damaged in the 1829 earthquake, is behind the castle walls on the *El Castell hill*. Guardamar del Segura caught the eyes of property speculators at the end of the 20th century. The countless restaurants, bars and terrace cafés on the attractive promenades (*Av. d'Europa, Paseo Maritimo*) that run parallel to the *Platja Centre*, the central beach, are pleasant places to stop and take a break. In summer, night owls flock to *Cine+Copas*.

Travellers with a limited budget should check into the *Hotel Eden Mar (25 rooms | C/. Mediterráneo 19 | tel. 9 65 72 92 13 | www.hoteledenmar.com | Budget)*; the four-star *Hotel Parque Mar (57 rooms | C/. Gabriel Miró s/n | tel. 9 66 72 51 72 | www.hotelparquemar.com | Moderate)*, with restaurant, will satisfy the more demanding. Guardamar del Segura is also popular with campers, offering a wide range of facilities: the *Marjal camping site (Marjal Complejo Turístico | Carretera Nacional 332, km 73.4 | tel. 9 66 72 70 70 | www.campingmarjal.com)* is open throughout the year and also rents out 40 bungalows. *Tourist office: Pl. de la Constitució 7 | tel. 9 65 72 44 88 | www.guardamar.net*

NOVELDA (124 C6) (*m̨ D9*)

Set against a background of barren, rugged hills that appear to be straight out of a Western, the area around Novelda (pop. 8000; ca. 15 km/9mi north-west), which is famous for its marble works, gives visitors a good impression of what life is like in the Spanish countryside. The cultural ensemble offered by the *La Mola* castle and *Santa María Magdalena Sanctuary* 3km (2mi) out of Novelda at the foot of the 541m (1775ft)-high Mola Peak is much more interesting than the city centre itself: you can reach both by follow-

LOW BUDGET

▶ ● Several museums in Alacant do not charge entrance fees. The *Museo de Arte Contemporáneo (Pl. de Santa María 3 | Tue–Sat 10am–8pm, Sun 10am–2pm)* has exhibitions of modern and contemporary art; ornate Nativity cribs are on display in the *Museo de Belenes (C/. San Agustín 3 | July/Aug Mon 6–9pm, Tue–Fri 11am–2pm and 6–9pm, Sat 11am–2am, at other times Mon 5–8pm, Tue–Fri 10am–2pm and 5–8pm, Sat 10am–2pm.*

▶ As an alternative to the hotels, there are at least ten camping sites in the Benidorm area; they include the first-class *Almafra Resort (Partida de Cabut 25 | tel. 9 65 88 90 75 | www.campingalmafra.es)*, with a restaurant, indoor swimming pool, fitness room and sauna. There are also permanent mobile homes (minimum stay: two nights).

ing the signs towards Castell and Santuari. The small restored ● *castle (daily 10am–2pm and 4–7pm, in summer 10am–2pm and 5–8pm | free admission)* dates back to the days of the Moors and has two massive towers. The neighbouring Magdalena

and city (pop. 103,000) are separated into quite distinct districts, some of which are less inspiring than others. However, the *Sea and Salt Museum (Museo del Mar y de la Sal | C/. Patricio Pérez 10 | Tue–Sat 10am–2pm and 4–9pm, Sun 10am–1.30pm)*, the

La Mola castle and the Sanctuario Santa María Magdalena high up on a hill near Novelda

sanctuary *(same opening times as the castle)* is a completely different affair; construction was begun in 1918 based on a project by José Sala. The result is an ornate building with marble, quarry stones and brick arched windows in the Catalan style of Art Nouveau *Modernisme.* The light flows into the rather unassuming interior through red-and-white glass and a hillock covered with cactuses slopes down in front of the forecourt.
Information: C/. Mayor 6 | Novelda | tel. 9 65 60 92 28 | www.novelda.es

TORREVIEJA (127 E3) (*ΩΩ D11*)

In this area around 35km (22mi) to the south, where fishing and salt mining have been core sources of income for centuries, the Costa Brava once again displays everything that makes it so attractive: beaches, a harbour, highlife in summer and a well-developed tourist infrastructure. The coast

Submarino S-61 Delfín (in summer Wed–Sun 5–9pm, at other times Wed–Sun 10am–1pm) that can be visited at the port and the cruises along the coast in excursion boats are all well worth a visit.
Accommodation can be found around 5km (3mi) to the north in the three-star Hotel *Cabo Cervera (186 rooms | Ctra. Torrevieja–La Mata s/n | tel. 9 66 92 17 17 | www.hotelcabocervera.com | Moderate)* with a pool and attractive off-season rates. Numerous restaurants, including those around *Pl. Capdepont,* will take care of all your creature comforts. Night owls head for the area near *C/. Ramón y Cajal.*
The 9150-acre *Parc Natural Lagunas de La Mata y Torrevieja* is located to the northwest of the city. The nature reserve consists of two large salt lagoons that are frequently visited by flamingos.
Tourist office: Pl. Capdepont s/n | tel. 9 65 70 34 33 | www.torrevieja.es

COSTA CÁLIDA/ MAR MENOR

Bays flanked by rugged rocks, spectacular ribbons of sand, crystal-clear water, secluded bathing spots – these are just some of the highlights of the Costa Cálida in the Murcia region. It hardly ever rains here; warm weather is guaranteed in the summer, and there are dozens of magnificent beaches and bays to choose from in the areas around Águilas and Mazarrón.

Tourists can find twice as much pleasure in the La Manga del Mar Menor holiday region. There are beaches and places to go swimming on both sides of their hotel: to the west, the inland sea Mar Menor and the Mediterranean to the east. The Murcia coast is extremely popular with water sports enthusiasts and families with children. Along with tourism, agriculture – especially lettuce, tomatoes and nectarines – play a major role here. The soil also produces apricots, grapes and peppers. Cartagena is an important harbour city, which encircles a large bay and has preserved many traces of its long history. The Carthaginians and Romans were among the earliest to feel at home here. The best overview of the city is from the hill of *Concepción* castle. It is worth making an excursion to the regional metropolis Murcia, the heart of the 4370mi² autonomous community. The entire region is

Photo: Kayakers on the Mar Menor

The Costa Cálida, the 'Hot Coast' – which includes the Mar Menor – really is a hot holiday tip

marked by fascinating contrasts between fertile valleys, the sea and desert-like areas.

ÁGUILAS

(126 B6) (*B13*) **The hottest spot on the 'Hot Coast' is Águilas (pop. 34,000), a town that has still managed to preserve much of its traditional charm.**

People still meet, just as they always have, in the bars and on the promenade for a chat, sit down and relax in the shade of the tropical greenery on the **INSIDER TIP** *Plaza de España* and enjoy the view of the harbour and the castle. However, once the carnival gets underway, normality is turned on its head! The locals really let their hair down, things almost get out of control and no cost or effort is spared to

The port of Águilas below the Castillo de San Juan

have a good time. No less than 100 *peñas*, groups of friends, uphold the old traditions; they start preparing their extravagant costumes in summer and inject the parades with the flair of the carnival in Brazil. Information and videos can be found under: *www.carnavaldeaguilas.org* Águilas looks back on an Imperial past, as can be seen in the ruins of the Roman baths on C/. Canalejas, and is certainly not a blank spot on the tourist map these days. There are around three dozen beaches and bays spread throughout the area. Protected by the Sierra del Cantar and Sierra de la Carrasquilla in the hinterland, the locals are proud to tell tourists that their city has an average annual temperature of 25°C (77°F) – the same temperature as Tenerife in the Canaries.

SIGHTSEEING

CASTILLO DE SAN JUAN DE LAS AGUILAS ✺

The fortress that dominates the town was built in the 16th century on the ruins of an earlier Moorish building to provide protection from pirates and renovated in the 18th century. At the time, there was a latent fear of being attacked by the Turks and Berbers. The fortress complex is divided into three sections and guarantees splendid views over the city and bay. *Tue–Sun 11am–1pm and 4–6pm (in summer 6–9pm) | above Plaza de España*

MUSEO ARQUEOLÓGICO

The archaeological museum displays a selection of amphorae and remnants of Roman bowls. *Mon 5–8pm (summer 6–9pm), Tue–Sat 10.30am–2pm and 5–8pm (summer 10am–1pm and 6–9pm), Sun 10am–1pm | C/. Conde de Aranda 8*

MUSEO DEL CARNAVAL

The carnival museum, which is almost hidden away in a residential building, exhibits a large number of highly imaginative costumes that give an impression of the carnival fun in Águilas! *Tue, Thu 10.30am–2pm and 5–8pm (July/Aug 10am–1pm and 6–9pm), Sat 10.30am–*

2pm (July/Aug 10am–1pm) | C/. Pizarro, Edificio La Torre

MUSEO DEL FERROCARRIL

The small railway museum is ideal for locomotive fanatics. Its collection includes historical photographs and tools, as well as model railways. *Mon–Sat 10am–noon and 4–6pm (July/Aug 10am–1pm and 5–8pm), Sun only 10am–noon (July/Aug 1pm) | Estación de Ferrocarril, Planta Sótano*

FOOD & DRINK

INSIDER TIP BAR DE FELIPE

This restaurant is an institution in Águilas and is very popular with the locals. It serves delicious tapas and other small dishes, including sardines and tuna. The speciality of the house is dried octopus *(pulpo seco)*. *Daily | Explanada del Puerto s/n | Budget*

INSIDER TIP CASA DEL MAR

This fish restaurant behind the port appears rather nondescript at first glance. Recommended starters include salads (*alcaparras*, capers, are a typical dish), or *raciones* of octopus *(pulpo)* or shrimps and garlic in oil *(gambas al ajillo)*. Depending on the day's catch, the main courses are sea bream *(dentón)* or sea bass *(lubina)*. The restaurant also serves rice dishes and the quality is excellent. *Closed Sun evening and Mon | Explanada del Puerto s/n | tel. 968412923 | Moderate*

LA VELETA

La Veleta is very popular with the locals on account of its specialities such as fried octopus *(pulpo frito)* and other tasty seafood. The daily set menu is a bit more elaborate than in many restaurants. *Closed Sun | C/. Blas Rosique 6 | tel. 968 411798 | Moderate*

BEACHES

⭐ Delightful and sandy: the *Playa de las Delicias* in the main bay between the port and the rock formations around the *Pico L'Aguilica*. The short climb up to the lookout point is well worth the effort. There are two other popular beaches in the vicinity: the *Playa de Poniente* and *Playa de la Colonia*; both are south-west of the castle hill and flanked by beautiful promenades. Further to the south-west, the main road in the direction of the Andalusian province of Almería leads to especially picturesque spots known as *Cuatro Calas,* the 'four bays' (including *Higuerica* and *Carolina*). There are other beaches and bays waiting to be explored on both sides of *Cabo Cope* north-east of the town; one of the loveliest is *Playa de Calabardina*.

SPORTS & ACTIVITIES

Diving courses, as well as night dives, are organised by the *Escuela de Buceo Estela (Paseo de Parra 38 | tel. 968448144 | www.escueladebuceo.com)*. You can hire

---

⭐ **Beaches in Águilas**
Promenade-lined beaches in the city, wonderful bays outside → p. 81

⭐ **Mazarrón**
What a wonderful choice of sandy coves → p. 83

⭐ **Mar Menor**
Vast lagoon: heaven for water sports enthusiasts → p. 83

⭐ **Murcia Cathedral**
Stronghold of the faith in the heart of the city → p. 89

MARCO POLO HIGHLIGHTS

Bizarre works of art created by nature: Erosiones de Bolnuevo near Mazarrón

bicycles from *Mountain Bike (C/. Barcelona 1 | tel. 9 68 41 39 84)*. There are paths for joggers and hikers that run for miles along the coast to the *Cuatro Calas* south-west of the Poniente Beach

ENTERTAINMENT

Concerts of every kind are held either in the *Casa de Cultura,* the municipal culture centre named after Águila's most famous son the actor Francisco Rabal or in the *Auditorio C/. Isaac Peral.*

WHERE TO STAY

APARTAMENTOS ÁGUILAS DE LOS COLLADOS

Complex with 87 well-equipped holiday flats (three types), each with kitchen and air conditioning. There is a pleasant pool. *Urbanización Los Collados | tel. 9 68 41 91 00 | Moderate*

CAMPING BELLAVISTA

Small camping site a short way away; it also possible to hire permanently installed mobile homes. The guests like to get together in the terrace bar in summer. *Carretera Vera, km 3 | tel. 9 68 44 91 51 | www.campingbellavista.com | Budget*

MAYARÌ

Small, family-run hotel with charm north-east of Águilas in Calabardina. Perfect for guests looking for peace and quiet. The room price includes breakfast. *8 rooms | C/. Rio de Janeiro 14 | Calabardina | tel. 9 68 41 97 48 | www.hotel-mayari.com | Moderate*

EL PARAÍSO

Functional two-star house a little way out of town near the Playa de Calabardina on

the road to Cabo Cope. Breakfast is included in the price of the room. *30 rooms | Ctra. Cabo Cope s/n | Calabardina | tel. 9 68 41 94 44 | www.hotelelparaiso.net | Budget*

PUERT JUAN MONTIEL

The best hotel in Águilas, directly on the seaside promenade and near the beach, with an unimpaired view as far as the castle hill. Includes a beautiful spa, restaurant, pool and fitness room. Luxurious and spacious architecture that has been awarded four stars. *128 rooms | Av. del Puerto Deportivo 1 | Playa de Poniente | tel. 9 68 49 34 93 | www.hotelpuertojuan montiel.com | Moderate–Expensive*

Pl. de Antonio Cortijos s/n | tel. 9 68 49 32 85 | www.aguilas.es

WHERE TO GO

MAZARRÓN ★ (126 C5) (*C12*)
The next highlight on the Costa Cálida is Mazarrón (pop. 30,000) about 60km (37mi) to the north-east. The town is split between the coastal zone *Puerto de Mazzarón* and a small district around 5km (3mi) inland. The real attraction is the coast with its string of sandy bays and a  INSIDER TIP lookout point *(mirador)* between the *Playa de la Pava* and *Playa de la Reya* offering spectacular views. The lengthy *Castellar* and *Bolnuevo* beaches are very popular. The *Erosiones de Bolnuevo,* bizarrely eroded formations carved by the wind and weather, are a short distance away from the Bolnuevo beach. There are designated areas for naturists, *calas nudistas,* to the south-east. Open-air concerts are held occasionally in summer (on the *Playa del Puerto* and at other locations). You will find decent accommodation in the three-star *Hotel Bahia (53 rooms | Playa de la Reya | tel. 9 68 59 40 00 | www.hotelbahia.net | Budget). Oficina de Turismo* in Puerto de Mazarrón *(Pl. Toneleros 1 | tel. 9 68 59 44 26 | www.mazarron.es)*.

LA MANGA DEL MAR MENOR

(127 E4–5) (*D12*) **Holiday region around the 'Little Sea', the ★ Mar Menor lagoon. The Salinas de San Pedro del Pinatar follow to the north and there is a series of villages like Los Narejos**

There is hardly ever a lack of space on the beaches of La Manga del Mar Menor

and Los Alcázares on the west side; that is also where Murcìa's San Javier Airport is located.

With an area of 50mi², the Mar Menor is more than twice the size of Loch Ness and is considered the largest coastal lagoon in Europe. Appeals to forbid motorised water sports on the inland sea for ecological reasons have so far fallen on deaf ears. There is still not a strong lobby for environmental protection in Spain, although many of the species of fish and the seahorse population in the Mar Menor are in urgent need of protection.

A legend about a king's daughter surrounds the tower which can be seen on the *Isla Mayor*, the largest island and one that is private property. Her father supposedly kept her imprisoned there after he had refused to let her marry a commoner and she died of a broken heart. According to local lore, when it is full moon, one can still hear eerie laments …

The high-speed approach road is not the only reason for most holidaymakers heading directly to the unique geographical feature 'the sleeve', *La Manga,* which has become a synonym for summer fun. The 'sleeve' is a narrow 18.5km (11.5mi) spit of land that separates the Mar Menor from the Mediterranean. La Manga del Mar Menor, to give the town its full name,

(pop. 5000) sprawls over the entire length of the spit and is crammed with villas and nondescript blocks of flats. It enjoys an excellent reputation as a paradise for water sports enthusiasts, and kitesurfers can be seen streaking across the Mar Menor while divers throw themselves into the waves of the Mediterranean. In summer, the number of people in the area mushrooms.

The main road *Gran Vía* cuts through the 'sleeve' and addresses are usually indicated by the kilometre (e.g. 'km 5') or appropriate exit (*salida*, e.g. 'salida 37'); the numbering begins at the only access road to the 'sleeve' and runs from south to north. La Manga del Mar Menor is the starting and finishing point for fascinating tours through the region of Murcia *(see 'Trips & Tours')*. However, the vast Mar Menor is anything but an insiders' tip. There are around 20,000 guest beds and around one million people from Spain and abroad visit the area each year.

SIGHTSEEING

CABO DE PALOS ⚓

A cape with a lighthouse that juts out on the south-eastern point of the 'sleeve'. There is a beautiful view over the sea and La Manga from the platform in front of

SUNKEN SHIPS

It was a bright sunny day in August 1906 when the 'Sirio', which was on route from Genoa to South America, met its Waterloo near the Islas Hormigas ('Ant Islands'). The trans-Atlantic steamer ran, full speed, into the *Bajo de Fuera*, a rock 3.5 m (11.5 ft) below the surface of the water. There were 765 passengers and 127 crew members on board. The captain was one of the first to leave the sinking ship; panic broke out and 440 people perished in this accident. In 1917, the 'Standfield', a British merchant ship, sank not far away, when it was torpedoed by a German submarine.

Fishermen in the port of Cabo de Palos by the Mar Menor

the lighthouse. Restaurants, diving school operators and a small information centre (*Centro de Interpretación*; easy to miss) are located around the marina basin on *Paseo del Puerto*. Life on Cabo de Palos is far more traditional, and it not nearly as built up as elsewhere on the 'sleeve'.

FOOD & DRINK

DI MARE
Pleasant pizzeria nestled in the atmosphere of the marina – enjoyable spot with a terrace. *Daily | Puerto Deportivo Tomás Maestre | tel. 9 68 14 02 00 | Budget*

EL PEZ ROJO ⭐
This traditional restaurant has a wonderful view of the sea. Fish and seafood galore are best 'washed down' with the excellent wines from Jumilla. The choice *menú de degustación* (for at least two

persons) will please even sophisticated diners. Enjoy your aperitif at the small bar near the entrance before you sit down to eat. *Closed Mon | Paseo Marítimo | Cabo de Palos | tel. 9 68 56 31 09 | Moderate– Expensive*

LA TANA
Fish and rice dishes set the tone in this restaurant. The meal of the day is very popular and there are also more elaborate – and, naturally, more expensive – options. The terrace at the port is open if the weather is fine – and it usually is here. *Daily | Cabo de Palos | Paseo de la Barra | tel. 9 68 56 30 03 | www.la-tana.com | Moderate–Expensive*

BEACHES

There are spacious beaches on the Mediterranean (wider and more continuous) and on the Mar Menor side. The gradual decline from the beach into the 'Little Sea', where the water reaches a maximum depth of 7m (23ft), makes it particularly suitable for families with small children.

SPORTS & ACTIVITES

Diving courses and special excursions for cracks, sometimes with adventurous dives at night and to wrecks, are organised by *Planeta Azul (Paseo del Puerto s/n | Cabo de Palos | tel. 9 68 56 45 32 | www.planeta-azul.com)* and *Islas Hormigas (Paseo de la Barra 15 | Cabo de Palos | tel. 9 68 14 55 30 | www.islashormigas.com)*.
Sailing and windsurfing (courses as well as equipment hire) are the business of the *Escuela de Vela Sandrina (Gran Vía, km 5,3, Edificio Orfeo | La Manga del Mar Menor | tel. 9 68 14 13 27 | www.escuela sandrina.com)* and the *Escuela de Vela Manga Surf (Gran Vía | Acceso Isla de Ciervo | tel. 9 68 14 53 31 | www.mangasurf. com)*.

ENTERTAINMENT

The most popular places to spend the evening hours are around the *Tomás Maestre Marina (Gran Vía, km 14)* and near *Zoco de Levante (Gran Vía, salida 37)*.

WHERE TO STAY

CAMPING-CARAVANING LA MANGA
It is also possible to hire bungalows for up to six persons at this year-round camping site. The complex is located a few miles from the entrance to the 'sleeve'. *Autovía de La Manga, salida 11 | tel. 9 68 56 30 14 | www.caravaning.es |* Budget

BOOKS & FILMS

▶ **Duende: A Journey in Search of Flamenco** – This much acclaimed auto-biography-cum-travelogue by Jason Webster recounts of the author's quest to discover *duende* – that strong state of emotion and expression thought to be captured in flamenco. Like his sub-sequent books, much of the action takes place on the Costa Blanca.

▶ **A Late Dinner: Discovering the Food of Spain** – If you still think that the only thing the Spanish can cook is paella, then Paul Richardson's book will be very enlightening. In a humorous and well-observed study of Spanish food and culture, the author reveals some of the country's culinary secrets.

▶ **El Cid** – At the latest when Hollywood star Charlton Heston alias El Cid rides past the walls of Peñíscola, you will realise that you were once there yourself. Anthony Mann filmed the mediaeval classic on the coast in 1961 with Sophia Loren and Raf Vallone in other main roles.

▶ **The Cold Light of Day** – This 2012 thriller about a man whose family is kidnapped in Spain on a sailing holi-day received mixed reviews. True, it is not the best film ever made with Sigourney Weaver and Bruce Willis, but it does include some spectacular shots of Alicante and La Granadella Bay.

View over the harbour bay of Cartagena

LA MANGA CLUB HOTEL PRÍNCIPE FELIPE

This hotel to the south of Mar Menor offers top-class accommodation; there are several restaurants and golf courses on the gigantic complex. The ● ☆ INSIDER TIP *Spa La Manga Club* is a luxurious oasis of health, with sauna, steam bath, indoor swimming pool, whirlpool – and the additional bonus of a spectacular view of the Mar Menor through the panoramic windows. *192 rooms | Los Belones | tel. 9 68 33 12 34 | www.lamangaclub.com | Expensive*

INSIDER TIP VILLAS LA MANGA

This well cared-for complex provides attractively designed self-catering holiday flats that are suitable for a maximum of three adults or two adults and two children (up to around 11 years of age). They are equipped with a small kitchen, and the large car park in front of the house makes them ideal for holidaymakers with the car. The pool and lovely sunbathing lawns make up for it not being directly on the beach. *Closed mid-Dec–beginning of Feb | 60 units| Gran Vía | km 3 | tel. 9 68 14 52 22 | www.villaslamanga.es | Moderate*

INFORMATION

Las Amoladeras | Gran Vía, km 0 | tel. 9 68 14 61 36 | www.marmenor.es

WHERE TO GO

CARTAGENA (127 D5) (𝄞 D12)

This harbour town (pop. 215,000), located 30km (19mi) to the south-west has a rich history that extends back more than 2000 years. Although over the years much of the ancient architecture has had to make way for new buildings, one can still see remains of the stone streets and Punic city wall *(Muralla Púnica,* with information centre and entrance to the monastery crypt from the 18th century, *July–mid-Sep daily 10am–2.30pm and 4–8.30pm, Nov–March Tue–Sun 10am–5.30pm, at other times Tue–Sun 10am–*

2.30pm and 4–7.30pm | C/. San Diego 25) and the archaeological park of *Cerro Molinete*. Traces of life during Roman times are visible in the *Casa de la Fortuna*, a residential building from the 1st century BC with its mosaic flooring *(Tue–Sun 10am–2/2.30pm, in summer 10am–2.30pm and 4–8.30pm | entrance on Pl. del Risueño)*, in the Augusteum where the clergy met in the 1st and 2nd centuries AD *(C/. Caballero; July–mid-Sep Tue–Sun 10am–2.30pm, Nov–March Tue–Sun 2–5.30pm, at other times Tue–Sun 4–7.30pm)*, in the *Archaeological Museum (C/. Ramón y Cajal 45 | Tue–Fri 10am–2pm* and 5–8pm, Sat/Sun 11am–2pm | www. museoarqueologicocartagena.es) and in the *Teatro Romano (May–Sep Tue–Sat 10am–8pm, at other times 10am–6pm, Sun always 10am–2pm | C/. Dr. Tapia Martínez s/n, next to the Muralla Bizantina)*; the theatre once accommodate 6000 spectators. The ⚜ castle hill with the *Castillo de la Concepción (July–mid-Sep daily 10am–2.30pm and 4–8.30pm, Nov–March Tue–Sun 10am–5.30pm, at other times Tue–Sun 10am–2.30pm and 4–7.30pm)* offers the best views of the theatre, docks and surrounding mountains. The hills that can be easily reached by a panoramic lift *(ascensor panorámico)* are the coolest part of the city in summer and thus very popular with the locals; the operating times of the lift are coordinated with those of the castle. At the station at the bottom of the ⚜ panoramic lift, you will see the entrance to a former bunker from the Spanish Civil War – now a museum *(Refugio-Museo de la Guerra | July–mid-Sep daily 10am–2.30pm and 4–8.30pm, Nov–March Tue–Sun 10am–5.30pm, at other times Tue–Sun 10am–2.30pm and 4–7.30pm | C/. Gisbert)*. The seaside, with its restaurants and cafés, is a popular place for people to get together in the evening and is also where the 'Barco Turístico' departs on tours of the harbour during the day. *Information: Oficina de Turismo | Palacio Consistorial | Pl. del Ayuntamiento 1 | tel. 9 68 12 89 55 and 9 68 50 00 93 | www. cartagenaturismo.es, www.cartagena puertodeculturas.com*

LOW BUDGET

▶ Admission to the Museum for Modern Art in Cartagena is free of charge *(Museo Regional de Arte Moderno | Palacio de Aguirre | Pl. de la Merced 15 | Tue–Sat 11am–2pm and 5–8pm, Sun 11am–2pm)*.

▶ ● You can also visit the *Museo Nacional de Arqueología Subacuática (mid-April–Mid-Oct Tue–Thu 10am–9pm, Fri/Sat 10am–10pm, at other times Tue–Sat 10am–7.30pm, Sun always 10am–3pm | Paseo Alfonso XII 22 | museoarqua.mcu.es)*, with treasures salvaged from the sea including amphorae and ivory from Roman and Phoenician times, free of charge after 2pm on Saturday and all day Sunday.

▶ There is a street market *(mercadillo)* on Sunday morning near *C/. Parque de Doñana* in Puerto de Mazarrón where a wide variety of clothing, shoes and fruit is sold.

MURCIA (127 D3) *(f C11)*
▦ MAP INSIDE BACK COVER
The regional capital (pop. 350,000), 75km (47mi.) north-west of La Manga del Mar Menor on the Rio Segura, is in the midst of a large fruit and vegetable growing region. The town can look back on

Construction of Murcia's spectacular Cathedral began at the end of the 14th century

1200 years of history. Its first rulers were the Moors who enclosed the settlement within a massive mantle of walls, named it Mursiya and were in control until well into the 13th century. The Christians then moved in and, in 1394, began construction of the magnificent ⭐ *Cathedral*, which is still Murcia's most important architectural monument. Its 90m (295 ft)-high tower is the symbol of the city. The architectural styles of the house of worship display both Gothic and Baroque styles; the interior decoration of the *Capilla de los Vélez* is particularly extravagant.

There are attractive gardens towards the river near the Cathedral. A visit to the *Museo Salzillo (in summer only Mon–Sat 10am–2pm, at other times Mon–Sat 10am–5pm and Sun 11am–2pm | Pl. de San Agustín 3 | www.museosalzillo.es)* in the Eremita de Jesús with a comprehensive exhibition from the oeuvre of the local Baroque sculptor Francisco Salzillo (1707–1783) is especially worthwhile. The Museum of Fine Arts *(Museo de Bellas Artes | C/. Obispo Frutos 12 | Tue–Fri 10am–2pm and 5–8pm, Sat 11am–2pm and 5–8pm, Sun 11am–2pm)* focuses on paintings from the Renaissance and Baroque periods.

Murcia's appeal is not only due to its many cultural attractions. The local population is fond of celebrating and the number of young people studying here guarantees that the city is always full of life. Plaza Santo Domingo, Plaza Cardinal Belluga and Plaza de las Flores with excellent tapas bars are among the most boisterous areas. There are also tasty titbits and a daily set menu in the café-bar *Roses & Rosell (daily | Plaza de Camachos 16 | tel. 9 68 93 39 70 | Budget)*. The four-star hotel *Rosa Victoria (80 rooms | Av. del Rocío 2 | tel. 9 68 27 28 29 | www.hotelrosavictoria.com | Budget)* provides modern, reasonably-priced accommodation.

Information: *Pl. Cardenal Belluga s/n |tel. 9 68 35 87 49 | www.turismodemurcia.es*

TRIPS & TOURS

The tours are marked in green in the road atlas, the pull-out map and on the back cover

1 HIKING IN THE SERRA D'IRTA NATURE RESERVE

The Serra d'Irta (also: Sierra de Hirta) Nature Reserve south of Peñíscola guarantees hikers a wealth of new experiences. It is essential to get an overview map of the area – which is usually also available in English – before you set off. After a short drive to the starting point, a 17km (10.5mi), (4–5 hour)-hike between the coastline and mountains lies ahead of you. The level of difficulty is given as 'medium' but it can be rather strenuous. Be sure not to forget: water, food, sun protection, good shoes and your swimming gear! You should count on the tour taking a full day and set off early in the morning.

Take the southern exit from the centre of **Peñíscola** → p. 38 and follow the brown signs to the nature reserve. After around 3.5km (2mi), park your car at the turn-off to the left – on a cleared piece of ground. From here, the path goes towards **Torre Abadum** (also *Abadun* or *Badun*, 2km/1mi) and **Playa Pebret** (4.1km/2.5mi). A stretch of asphalt is followed by a track that is also occasionally used by cars. This wide gravel road rises upwards over impressive coastal landscapes, remains

Photo: Plaza España in Lorca

Under the spell of mountains and coasts: a colourful mix of tours through nature reserves, to old cultures and 'young' towns

on the crest for a while and then leads past the Moorish Abadum (10th century)-watchtower, which is clearly visible from a distance. This was once used to look out for pirates. If you have an off-road vehicle or feel confident enough to drive up the gravel path in a normal car – something many people do – you can shorten your hike and park here. There is a surfaced stretch down from the round tower through a grove of pine trees that then runs into a path to the right a few hundred metres before Playa Pebret. A signpost points in the direction of the next waypoint, the Mas del Senyor rest area 3.5km (2mi) away. You now move away from the coast and tackle the most arduous section of the trail. The path is narrow, steep and stony and rises continuously upwards. Looking back, you can see the Mediterranean;

The tour begins and ends in pretty Peñíscola

looking forward, the higher elevations of the Sierra appear behind a small ridge. The track takes you past derelict houses and then across a field of scree. A electricity pylon shows that civilisation is not far away and, near a bright country house and clearly signposted, the path turns to the left onto a wider track. From this junction, it is only 1500m to **Mas del Senyor** and 2.7km (1.7mi) to **Pou del Moro**. The path now becomes as wide as a normal road and is used by the people living on the scattered farms in the area. The landscape is otherwise almost completely untouched. You can hear dogs barking in the distance, and there is the aroma of pine trees and herbs in the air. French and butterfly lavender, as well as thyme, rosemary and sage, flourish in the nature reserve. When you reach the rest area at **Mas del Senyor** you can enjoy a well-earned break at one of the picnic tables in the shade of the trees and listening to the artificially created brook babbling nearby.

There are now only 1200m to **Pou del Moro**, the 'Moors' Fountain'; it is not on the main path but worth the little detour. From here, the wide dirt track makes its way up and down through pine groves and, in a wide curve, leads 4km (2.5mi) down to the coast. Although you will frequently come across yellow-and-white hiking signs (and sometimes tall wooden posts with red marks at the top), there is one occasion – when you reach a crossroads where three paths meet – that you will not immediately know which path to take; you should take the one to the left. The path gradually leads towards the sea and reaches the track near the coast. It is only a few hundred metres from this crossing to the **Pebret** and **Russo** beaches and you can take a well-deserved dip in the sea and cool off. Refreshed and fortified from your stop at Playa Pebret, you set off on the final 4.1km (2.5mi) past the ☆ **Torre Abadum** with the unobstructed view of **Peñíscola** until you reach the starting point once again. *www.sierrairta.com*

2 TOUR OF DISCOVERY THROUGH THE MURCIA REGION

 The holiday area around the Mar Menor is the starting point for a round trip of about 300km

(186mi). Depending to an extent on what you feel like doing, you should plan on it taking 2–3 days. The contrasts in the Murcia region provide the leitmotif for this journey: mountains and the sea, the beaches at Mazarrón and Águilas, the cities of Cartagena and Murcia. You can stay overnight in Mazarrón and Águilas. The tour starts and finishes in La Manga del Mar Menor → p. 83 where the motorway to Cartagena comes to an end; the mountains on the coast prevent it going any further. After 30km (19mi), you reach Cartagena → p. 87 , which – owing to its turbulent past – is also known as the *Puerto de Culturas* 'Port of Cultures'. On account of its strategic location – with a protected harbour and fortifications on the surrounding hills – nobody was ever able to conquer Cartagena from the sea. The city was founded in 227 BC by the Carthaginian General Hasdrubal, Hannibal's brother. The Carthaginians were defeated shortly thereafter by the Romans, and this is celebrated every year in the second half of September in the *Fiestas de Cartagineses y Romanos* – a fabulous costume festival! The Apostle James is also said to have landed in Cartagena to start his missionary work in Spain. In 1931, King Alfonso XIII left Spain and went into exile from here. After a visit to the historical sites, such as the *Muralla Púnica* and the castle mountain *Concepción*, you should take a stroll through the pedestrian precinct on *C/. Mayor*: the *Restaurante Columbus (C/. Mayor 18 | tel. 9 68 50 10 68 | closed Sun in winter. | Budget–Moderate)* specialises in tapas, a daily set menu of the day and, the real highlight of the house, several ● INSIDER TIP paella variations. The *Principal Restaurant (C/. Príncipe de Vergara 2 | tel. 9 68 12 30 31 | So, closed Mon and Tue evenings | Budget–Moderate)* is the place to go for a more substantial meal; the menu lists an excellent selection of rice and fish dishes, as well as a reasonably priced daily set menu on weekdays. The final destination of your walk is the pleasantly laid-out seaside promenade where you will find many cafés; it is also the starting point for tours of the harbour *(see 'Travel with Kids')*. There, you will also see a forerunner of the submarine, as conceived by the engineer Isaac Peral (1851–95) from Cartagena, in a pool surrounded by fountains.

The main road makes its way through the mountainous countryside, reaching an elevation of 352m (1155ft) at the La Cuesta Pass. For a while, visitors have the impression that they have reached one of the most remote sections of Spain, but the greenhouses and blocks of flats in Mazarrón → p. 83 soon bring them back down to earth. The town's key attraction

The Carthaginian Hasdrubal is considered to be the founder of Cartagena

Murcia's modern town hall is in stark contrast to the Old Town

is the **Puerto de Mazarrón** stretch of coast 5km (3mi) away from the main part of town. This coast of what was one a mining area is famous for its lovely beaches and bays, as well as its diving area and the interesting rock formations *Erosiones del Bolnuevo*. Mazarrón is a good place to spend the night; decent accommodation is available in the *Hotel La Cumbre (121 rooms | Urbanización La Cumbre | tel. 9 68 59 48 61 | www.hotellacumbre.com | Budget–Moderate)*.

The almost 60km (37mi) drive along the winding road between the coast and the inland cordillera takes you to the port and castle town of **Águilas → p. 79**, where you will find more excellent beaches and bays. In Águilas, there is a choice of two fairly long walks along the promenade: to the west, to the lookout point *Pico L'Aguilica* or to the *Playa de Poniente* to the west. After leaving Águilas, you travel for almost 40km (25mi) through a barren mountainous region until you reach **Lorca** (pop. 80,000). The mediaeval castle and some churches bear witness to the town's monumental heritage, and its Easter festivities

are famous throughout the country. It is here that there was a severe earthquake not long ago in 2011.

The N-340/A-7 makes its way past fertile fields of fruit and vegetables, as well as desert-like mountains, to **Murcia → p. 88**, 70km (43mi) away. As there is nothing of interest on the way, you should make your way directly to Murcia. There is, however, a pleasant place to stay for those who like rustic country hotels in the **Sierra Espuña** Nature Reserve 15km (9mi) north-west of **Alhama de Murcia**: the INSIDERTIP *Hospedería Bajo el Cejo (11 rooms | C/. El Paso | El Berro | tel. 9 68 66 80 32 | www. bajoelcejo.com | Moderate)*.

When you reach Murcia, you should park your car in the Barrio del Carmen and walk over the *Puente Viejo* bridge into the Old Town. In the town the Moors called Mursiya (pop. 350,000) everything revolves around the Cathedral; construction was begun in the 14th century and in some sections the exuberant Baroque decoration is almost overpowering. There are several cafés and the *tourist information office (Pl. Cardenal Belluga s/n | tel.*

968 35 87 49 | www.turismodemurcia.es) on the square in front of the Cathedral. The extensive pedestrian precinct reaches as far as Plaza Santo Domingo and is often full of high-spirited student life. INSIDER TIP Interesting processions are held in Murcia during the Holy Week. It is then only 75km (47mi) back to La Manga del Mar Menor.

EXPLORING THE SERRA D'ESPADÀ NATURE RESERVE

A beautiful mountainous route leads through the Serra d'Espadà Nature Reserve in the southern hinterland of the Costa del Azahar. The gateway to the reserve is La Vall d'Uixó where you can start off by visiting the St Joseph's Grottos. The route then does a loop through green mountain regions via Chóvar, Eslida and Tales. The attractive drive ends in Onda. You should plan a half or full day for this trip, depending on where you start or finish and how long you spend visiting caves and having lunch: the core stretch from la Val d'Uixó to Onda is around 35km (22mi) long.

The drive starts at the edge of La Vall d'Uixó and leads into the cavernous gloom of the flooded Coves de Sant Josep/Grutas de San José (see 'Travel with Kids'). Visitors are punted around in barges and also have to walk a short distance. Young and old are enchanted by the illuminated stalactites and stalagmites and curtains of rock. After this journey to the bowels of the earth, you can fortify yourself near the grotto. In the La Gruta Restaurant (Closed Mon | Paraje San José | tel. 964 66 00 08 | www.restaurantelagruta.com | Expensive), you can enjoy a pleasant daily set menu under the arches of the caves; there is also a good wine list.

After your meal, follow the signposts on the curvy little CV-230 road to the Parc Natural Serra d'Espadà. The 76,600-acre conservation area provides a strong contrast to the scenery on the coast and reaches a height of 1106m (3629ft) at the Pico de la Rápita. You drive past olive trees and orange plantation at the beginning of the tour; the rock formations in the distance look like sharks' fins. The drive up to the 400m (1312ft)-Marinet Pass starts behind Alfondeguilla. After a lengthy descent, you follow the right turn-off on the CV-219 towards Chóvar and Eslida. The area here is sparsely inhabited. Mountain silhouettes overlay each other, and the ensemble of houses in the village of Chóvar stand out against the backdrop of a mountain peak. There is another steep climb behind Chóvar. Green becomes the predominant colour once again, now interspersed with touches of yellow from the broom bushes and the rusty red of the cork oaks whose bark has been peeled off. You will start to feel a slight chill in the car when you reach ⛰ Port d'Eslida at an altitude of 620 m (2034 ft); on dull days clouds swirl around the peaks of the mountains. Take advantage of the car park at the top of the pass to rest a while and enjoy the pristine air.

Pine trees, moss-covered rocks and hairpin bends will be your companions all the way down over several levels until you reach the village of Eslida in the valley. You will see mountains wherever you look. The landscape becomes greener again between Eslida and Aín; from Aín (follow signpost towards Almedíjar) the road continues via L'Alcúdia de Veo. The pines are now joined by olive and eucalyptus trees during the final mountain and valley stretch. The mountains start to lose their force behind Tales and the landscape becomes less attractive. The castle village Onda is no longer within the borders of the nature reserve; from there, you drive to the east and reach the coast motorway and the N-340.

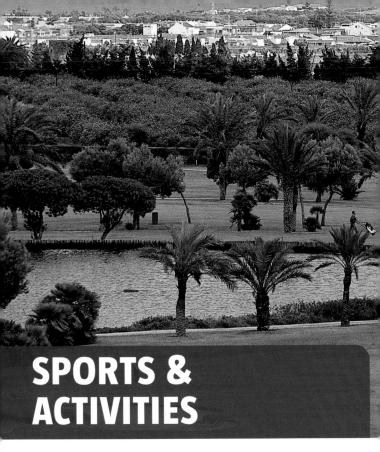

SPORTS & ACTIVITIES

Do you want to dive down to a shipwreck, take a sailing course or just paddle a kayak across the Mar Menor? The Spanish Mediterranean coast offers something for every sports enthusiast.

The Costa Blanca has also established itself as a popular destination for golf lovers.

BALLOONING

Aeroglobo (tel. 9 66 63 74 01 | www.aero globo.com) lies south of Elx; the balloon rides start in the morning on weekends and reach heights of 500m (1640ft); you are told where to meet when you make your reservation. The prices include a diploma

and picnic. Further inland, Bocairent, north-west of Alcoi, is the home base of *Tot Globo (Els Clots s/n | tel. 6 29 61 18 89 | www.totglobo.com).*

CYCLING

Cycling cannot be recommended everywhere in Spain: the cycle paths are often either in poor condition or do not exist at all; this, together with the heavy traffic and often inconsiderate drivers tend to reduce the pleasure of cycling in town. On the other hand the INSIDER TIP *Vías Verdes*, 'Green Routes' that run along the old, disused railway lines are lovely; these include

Photo: Los Belones golf course

Balloning, hiking, bicycling or water sports – there are no limits to the activities you can enjoy here

the *Vía Verde de Ojos Negros II* covering close to 68km (42mi) between Barracas (Castellón Province) and Algimia de Alfara (Valencia Province). Shorter stretches can be found in Alicante Province with the *Vía Verde de Maigmó* between Agost and the 660m (2165ft)-high Puerto del Maigmó (22km/14mi), as well as the *Vía Verde del Xixarra 2* between the Santuario de las Virtudes and Biar (15 km/9mi). Mountain-bikers will like the route near the coast through the Serra d'Irta Nature reserve from Peñíscola to Alcossebre/Alcocebre. Spanish law requires cyclists to wear a helmet. *www.viasverdes.com*

DIVING

Dive down into the crystal-clear water to explore the surprisingly intact marine animal and plant world, in which it is even possible to observe rays, moray eels and sunfish. There are many diving schools on the Costa Blanca, which offer dives and provide courses at all levels. These include the *Centro de Buceo Greenwich* near Altea *(Puerto Deportivo Luis Campomanes | Edificio Comodoro | tel. 9 66 88 14 57 | www. greenwichdiving.com)* and the *Centro de Buceo Dive & Dive (Club Naútico | Av. del Puerto | tel. 9 65 83 92 70 | www.divedive company.com)*. The *Planeta Azul* diving centre *(Paseo del Puerto s/n | Cabo de Palos | tel. 9 68 56 45 32 | www.planeta azul.com)* organises various courses in the Mar Menor region; experienced divers can go down to see the INSIDER TIP wrecks around the Islas Hormigas.

GO-KARTING

There are several go-kart tracks on the coast. These include *Benikarts* near Benicàssim *(Ctra. Nacional 340, km 987 | tel. 9 64 30 36 03 | www.benikarts.com)*, *Karting La Vila* between Benidorm and La Vila Joiosa *(Ctra. Nacional 332-A, km 143 | tel. 9 65 89 46 76 | www.kartinglavila.es)* and the 1000m-course of the *Karting Club Finestrat (Ptda. La Foia Ampla | Finestrat | tel. 9 65 97 22 27 | www.kartingfinestrat.com)* near Benidorm. You can choose from several types of karts at the INSIDER TIP *La Manga Go-Kart* course *(Ctra. La Manga, km 19.2 | tel. 9 68 56 36 43 | www.lamangagokart. com)* near La Manga del Mar Menor.

GOLF

There are several 18-hole, par 72 courses near Alacant including the *Club de Golf Alenda* with its own golf school *(Autovía Alacant–Madrid, km 15 | Monforte del Cid | tel. 9 65 62 05 21 | www.alendagolf.com)*, the *Club de Golf Alicante (Av. Locutor Vicente Hipólito 37 | Playa de San Juan | tel. 9 65*

15 37 94 | www.alicantegolf.com) and *Lo Romeo Golf,* also with a golf academy, near Pilar de la Horadada *(Carretera Orihuela, km 29, CV 925 | Pilar de la Horadada | tel. 9 02 18 09 18 | www.loromerogolf.com)* and at other locations. The nine-hole course *Las Rejas Open Club Benidorm (Av. Vicente Pérez Devesa s/n | tel. 9 66 88 97 75 | www.lasrejasopenclub.com)* is in the urban area of Benidorm. You will find an excellent overview of the courses and their facilities under: www.golfcostablanca.org.

One of the most beautiful courses in Spain is located to the south of the Mar Menor: the INSIDER TIP *La Manga Club (Lomas Village | Los Belones | tel. 9 68 33 12 34 | www.lamangaclub.com)* with the *South Course* (6499m), *West Course* (5971m) and *North Course* (5753m). There are excellent trainers and courses at the golf academy.

HIKING

The most popular hiking areas are the nature reserves such as the *Serra d'Irta* where the paths are well marked. The *Sierra Helada* near Benidorm is an inviting area for long forays into the green; you can climb the *Penyal d'Ifac* in Calp, and explore the trails in the *El Montego Nature Reserve* behind Dénia.

KAYAKING

The *Escuela de Vela Sandrina (Gran Vía, km 5,3 | Edificio Orfeo | La Manga del Mar Menor | tel. 9 68 14 13 27 | www.escuela-sandrina.com)* has its headquarters on the shores of the Mar Menor. The school does not limit itself to sailing; it also rents out kayaks to people who want to explore a section of the inland sea on their own. Another recommended address is the kayak school run by the *Escuela de Pira-güismo Mar Menor (Explanada Barnuevo* s/n | Santiago de la Ribera | tel. 9 68 57 36 53 | piraguismomarmenor.com). The *Centro de Deportes Náuticos Las Antípodas (Ctra. Calp–Moraira, km 2 | tel. 9 65 83 83 10 | www.lasantipodas.com)* near Calp also rents kayaks and organises excursions.

PARACHUTING

The *Centro de Paracaidismo Skytime* on the Costa del Azahar near Castelló de la Plana *(Aeródromo El Pinar | Camino de la Plana s/n | tel. 6 05 92 03 80 | www.sky time.info)* offers tandem jumps from an altitude of 4000m (13,000ft) and intensive courses lasting several days.

SAILING

The sailing and boat clubs *(clubs náuticos)* sometimes organise sailing courses – occasionally for children from the age of 7. *Real Club Náutico de Calpe (Av. Puerto Pesquero s/n | Calpe | tel. 9 65 83 18 09 | www.rcnc.es)*, the *Club Náutico de Santa Pola (Muelle Poniente | Santa Pola | tel. 9 65 41 24 03 | www.cnauticosantapola.com)* and the *Real Club Náutico de Torre-*vieja *(Paseo Vistalegre s/n | Torrevieja | tel. 9 65 71 01 12 | www.rcnt.com)*. The sailing school run by the *Centro de Deportes Náuticos Las Antípodas (Ctra. Calp–Moraira, km 2 | tel. 9 65 83 83 10 | www.lasantipodas.com)* is located between Calp and Moraira. Many of the trainers only speak Spanish.

SURFING

Surfers will find what they are looking for at several places on the Costa Blanca including the area north-west of Dénia. The *La Chimenea-Les Deveses* region is famous for its strong winds (force 3.5–7). That is where you will also find the *Windcenter Dénia (Camí del Bassot | Playa Les Deveses | tel. 9 65 75 53 07 | www.windcenterdenia.com)*, which is open from Easter to Sept. The *Campello Surf Club (campellosurfclub.blogspot.com)* in El Campello north-east of Alacant also organises courses for beginners in summer. The Spanish Association of Nautical Destinations *(Asociación Española de Estaciones Naúticas | www.estacionesnauticas.info)* is a reliable source of information for surfers and other water sports enthusiasts.

There are many top spots for surfers on the coast

TRAVEL WITH KIDS

The Spanish like children. Nobody gets upset about noisy youngsters, even if it is late at night – children can do (just about) anything they want.

There are good playground facilities available, the tourist trains *(trens turísticos)* are fun, and – in the summer – water parks are very popular, albeit rather expensive.

COSTA DEL AZAHAR

COVES DE SANT JOSEP/GRUTAS DE SAN JOSÉ ★ ● (123 D5) (*∅ E–F5*)
Jump into the boat, keep your head down and then marvel at the bizarre stalactites and stalagmites as you glide along a sub-terranean river. Boatsmen punt you along passages and into cave chambers such as the 'Cathedral' and 'Bat Hall'. The most important nooks and crannies are illuminated and part of the tour ison foot. *Tour 40–45 min | daily 11am–1.15pm and 3.30–5.45pm, June/July, Sep to 6.30pm, Aug to 7.15pm | entrance fee 9.50 euros, children (4–13 years) 4.50 euros | on the out-skirts of La Vall d'Uixó, signposted access, large car park | www.riosubterraneo.com*

INSIDER TIP JARDÍN DEL PAPAGAYO (123 F2) (*∅ G3*)
Follow the wild screeching to the 'Parrot Garden'. The park-like area contains many

Photo: Children in costumes during the Fallas in Valencia

Parrots, elephants and stalactites – hardly a recipe for boredom! Caves, zoos and amusement parks await young explorers

aviaries, which you can enter – but beware of 'dive bombers'. If you buy a bag of food, some birds will eat out of your hand. At the end of the tour, visit the kangaroos in their special enclosure. The parrot's daredevil air shows are an additional attraction. *Daily 11am–8.30pm (summer), at other times until 5.30/6.30/7.30pm depending on the month | entrance fee 11.70 euros, children (3–12 years) 8.50 euros | Camino* *del Término Peñíscola–Benicarló (signposted from Peñíscola) | www.jardindel papagayo.com*

VALENCIA

AQUÓPOLIS CULLERA
(125 D2) *(◻ E–F7)*
The many highlights of the water park in Cullera range from the 'Mini Park' for the

young, and the 'Black Hole' and 'Kamikaze' for the brave. *Mid-June–beginning of Sep, July/Aug daily 11am–7pm, at other times daily 11am–6pm | entrance fee 21.50 euros, children from 0.90–1.40 m tall 17.50 euros (under 90cm free) | Ctra. Nazaret–Oliva | Cullera | www.cullera.aquopolis.es*

INSIDER TIP ▶ BIOPARC VALENCIA ☺
(125 D1) (*∅ E6*)
A little piece of Africa and even more – that is what the *Bioparc* offers. A new generation zoo that meets all the demands of the 21st century, Bioparc makes it possible for visitors to view the animals in authentically recreated habitats, in which they have plenty of space to move about. Rhinoceros, lions, giraffes, elephants, lemurs and several species of monkeys are just some of the animals you can see. The complex is located in the *Parque de Cabecera*, an extension of the *Jardines del Turia* park. *Daily from 10am to 9pm, April–Jun until to 8pm, at other times 6/7pm depending on the month | entrance fee 21.50, children (4–12 years) 16 euros | Av. Pío Baroja 3 | www.bioparcvalencia.es*

JARDINES DEL TURIA/
PARQUE GULLIVER (125 D1) (*∅ E6*)
Valencia's attractions for children are not limited to the *Bioparc,* the *Oceanogràfic* and the interactive *Science Museum (see p. 47).* The *Jardines del Turia, a park area* that was developed over a 7.5km (4.5mi)-area on the old river bed of the Riu Turia also includes the *Parque Gulliver* between the Palace of Music and City of the Arts and Sciences. There, you can see an enormous model of the legendary giant lying tied to the ground. His clothes form slides and other playground facilities. What is also nice is that no entrance fee is charged for the playground, but it is shut if the weather is bad. *July/Aug daily 10am–2pm and 5–9pm, at other times daily 10am–8pm*

COSTA BLANCA

AQUOPOLIS TORREVIEJA
(127 E3) (*∅ D11*)
Everyone slides into gear here! On the 'Kamikaze Slide', for instance, you zoom down into the refreshing water at a breathtaking pace. 'Speed' and 'Boomerang' are also guaranteed to increase your pulse rate. *Beginning of June–beginning of Sep daily 11am–7pm, at other times to 6pm | entrance fee 22.40 euros, children from 0.90–1.40 m tall 17.30 euros (under 90cm free) | Finca de la Hoya Grande | Torrevieja | www.torrevieja.aquopolis.es*

MUNDOMAR (125 E5) (*∅ F9*)
Animal park with lemurs, penguins, flamingos and other animals. The performances with sea lions, dolphins and parrots are the main attractions; shows usually at 11.15am, 2.30 and 3.30pm (parrots), 12.15 and 4.30pm (sea lions) and 1.30 and 5.45pm (dolphins); it is a good idea to check the current times on the park's homepage. The animals are also fed at different times and there is even a puppet theatre for younger children. In addition to the prices listed here, there are reduced rates in the afternoon *(entrada tarde)* and a combined ticket with the *Aqualandia* water park *(end of May–beginning of Oct | www.aqualandia.net). Feb–mid-Dec daily 10am–6pm, to 7/8pm depending on the season | entrance fee 25 euros, children (3–12 years) 20 euros | Sierra Helada s/n | Rincón de Loix, Benidorm | www.mundomar.es*

RÍO SAFARI ELCHE
(127 E–F2) (*∅ D–E10*)
Safari park with exotic animals from lemurs to giraffes in the shade of thousands of palm trees: the attractions include tours on the miniature railway, the crocodile farm and 'reptile cave' *(Cueva de los*

Reptiles). There are usually two shows a day with parrots, sea lions and an elephant. The complex also includes a swimming pool, which is open in summer. *In summer daily 10.30am–8pm, at other times 10.30am–6pm | entrance fee 20 euros, children (3–12 years) 15 euros | Ctra. Elx–Santa Pola | Polígono 1 | www.riosafari.com*

TERRA NATURA
(125 E5) (*[illmap] F9*)

Here, children will be able to come into (not too) close contact with more than 1500 animals including elephants, rhinoceros and predatory cats. The area is divided into individual sections such as 'America', 'Asia' and 'Pangea Volcano'. A combined ticket for Terra Natura and the *Aqua Natura* water park is available in summer. *March–Oct daily (depending on the month) 10am–5/6/7/8pm, Nov–Feb usually only Fri–Sun 10am–5/6pm | entrance fee 25 euros, children (4–12 years of age) 20 euros, additional entrance fee for 'Aqua Natura' water park 8 euros, combined ticket Terra Natura and Aqua Natura 33 euros, and 28 euros for children | Foia del Verdader 1 | Benidorm | www.terra natura.com*

COSTA CÁLIDA/MAR MENOR

TOUR OF THE PORT OF CARTAGENA ★ ● (127 D5) (*[illmap] D12*)

Enormous ships, yachts, container warehouses, the arsenal and the view of the mountains above the bay – tours in the *barco turístico* make it possible for visitors to experience the harbour town from the water. The trip lasts around 40–50 min, depending on whether the weather makes it possible to go to the entrance of the bay. As an extra, you can stop off to visit the fortress, the *Fuerte de Navidad* (19th century), and arrange to be picked up again one hour later. *Several trips daily, changing times, beginning of July–mid-Sep daily, no tours on Mon | Cartagena, departure form the central seaside promenade (Escala Real) | tickets 5.75 euros (with Fuerte de Navidad 8), children from 3–12 years 4.75 euros (with Fuerte de Navidad 6) | tel. 9 68 50 00 93 | www.cartagenapuerto deculturas.com*

Sunday trip: fun for the kids in the city park in Elx

FESTIVALS & EVENTS

If it's fiesta time, it's also time for bangers and fireworks. This is true even of the smallest villages where the festivals of the Patron Saint and ceremonious pilgrimages *(romerías)* are among the highlights of the year, as are the *Moros y Cristianos* (Moors and Christians) celebrations, which commemorate the Reconquista.

OFFICIAL HOLIDAYS

1 Jan: *Año Nuevo,* New Year's Day; **6 Jan:** *Reyes Magos,* Epiphany; **March/April:** *Viernes Santo,* Good Friday; **1 May:** *Fiesta del Trabajo,* Labour Day; **15 Aug:** *Asunción de Nuestra Señora,* Assumption; **12 Oct:** *Día de la Hispanidad,* Columbus Day; **1 Nov:** *Todos los Santos,* All Saints' Day; **6 Dec:** *Día de la Constitución,* Constitution Day; **8 Dec:** *Inmaculada Concepción,* Immaculate Conception; **25 Dec:** *Navidad,* Christmas Day

There are regional holidays, such as the *Día de San José* (St Joseph's Day, **19 March**), *Jueves Santo* (Maundy Thursday), *Lunes de Pascua* (Easter Monday) and *Día del Corpus* (Corpus Christi). Celebrations are also held in honour of the local patron

saints; for example, in Valencia **22 Jan** *San Vicente Mártir,* **1st Mon after Easter** *San Vicente Ferrer,* **9 Oct** is a regional holiday in Valencia.

FESTIVALS & EVENTS

JANUARY
5 Jan: Processions before ▶ *Epiphany* in Alacant, Dénia, Benicàssim, Elx, Benidorm; on the coast, the Three Wise Men often arrive onshore by boat

FEBRUARY/MARCH
▶ *Carnival* in Peñíscola, Alacant, Benidorm, Torrevieja and other locations; INSIDER TIP Águilas celebrates its carnival as a miniature version of Rio de Janeiro; *www.carna valdeaguilas.org*

MARCH
▶ ★ ● *Fallas:* in many towns and villages, enormous floats of wood and papier-mâché are set up and burned on St Joseph's Day (19 March) or in the night of the 20 March; all of this accompanied by a fireworks display *(see box on p. 53).* There is no topping the Fallas tradition in Valencia,

Explosive festivals: Hardly anywhere else in Spain are festivities celebrated with more bangs, fire and spectacle

but other towns such as Sagunt, Xàtiva, Benidorm and Burriana have plenty to offer, too.

▶ INSIDER TIP **Fiestas de la Magdalena:** City festival in Castelló de la Plana with processions, dancing and fireworks

MARCH/APRIL

Easter (▶ *Semana Santa)* with processions in many towns including Valencia, Alacant, Murcia, Cartagena, Elx, Lorca and Sagunt Around 23 April ▶ *Moros y Cristianos* in Alcoi

JUNE

On the evening before St John's Day (24 June) midsummer fire, ▶ *Hogueras de San Juan*, in Benidorm, Dénia and elsewhere

JULY

▶ *Fiestas Mayores Santísima Sangre*, Festival of the Patron Saint in Dénia

AUGUST

▶ ★ *Misteri d'Elx*, Mystery play in the Basilica Santa María; *www.misteridelx.com*
▶ *Tomatina*, Tomato fight in Bunyol (end of the month) during which more than 100 tons of tomatoes get thrown purely for fun, albeit dubious fun.

SEPTEMBER

▶ *Feria* in Murcia with folklore, ▶ *Moros y Cristianos*; *www.fiestasdemurcia.es*
In the second half of the month ▶ *Fiestas de Cartaginenses y Romanos*, the 'Festival of the Carthaginians and Romans' in Cartagena; *www.cartaginesesyromanos.es*

OCTOBER

Usually at the beginning of the month
▶ *Moros y Cristianos* in Benidorm

NOVEMBER

▶ *Patron Saint's festival* in Benidorm

LINKS, BLOGS, APPS & MORE

LINKS

▶ www.spain.info/en Official website of the Spanish Tourist Board. All you need to know about your destination at a glance, including comprehensive information about the main cities, beaches, accommodation, restaurants and events

▶ www.infocostablanca.com An informative and helpful website when planning your trip to Costa Blanca. There are maps of the region and of individual towns – and the gallery of photographs provides a stunning impression of what there is to see

▶ www.costablancaworld.com Useful website for people staying on the Costa Blanca for an extended period, with telephone numbers, advice regarding local services and details of what's on and where – and, of course, how to get there

▶ www.costa-news.com The website of Costa Blanca's local English-language newspaper *Costa Blanca News*. Founded in 1971 by Brian Sumner, the print version is published once a week on Friday and a selection of the news stories and all the classified advertisements are included on the website

▶ www.fallasfromvalencia.com Festive facts about the upcoming Fallas in Valencia

BLOGS & FORUMS

▶ http://lamarinaforum.com A general Costa Blanca forum for the English-speaking community on topics ranging from news sources to learning Spanish

▶ www.simplespanishfood.com A blog about Spanish food from an American perspective

▶ www.insidersabroad.com/spain/blogs A candid blog by various authors about life in Spain

▶ www.holavalencia.net English language city blog from Valencia; with permanently updated list of the top five sights, restaurants, 'things to do', etc, with city map, videos and forum

Regardless of whether you are still preparing your trip or already on the Costa Blanca: these addresses will provide you with more information, videos and networks to make your holiday even more enjoyable

VIDEOS

▶ www.spain-holiday.com/Costa-Blanca Travel video about the Costa Blanca, a bit too stereotyped but with fairly true-to-life impressions of the landscape and coast; in English

▶ www.valencia-cityguide.com/tour-ist-information/virtual-tour/valencia-video.html Unusual perspectives – Valencia from the air with background music. Titles show what can currently be seen

▶ www.telegraph.co.uk/telegraphtv/7511280/Las-Fallas-Valencias-festival-of-fire.html Exemplary impressions of the Fallas in Valencia, one of the largest festivals in Spain; in English accompanied by all of the noise of the fiesta

▶ www.youtube.com/watch?v=y9--c-NIUsE Personal travel report about Valencia, including scenes from the interior of the Cathedral and impressions of the *Fallas;* in English

APPS

▶ Valencia Map and Walking Tours Explore the city of Valencia, for the iPhone; special walks, city map with search function for the sights, restaurants etc.

▶ Costa Blanca Walks: An alternative for those who want to get away from the town for a while and hike in the mountains. Very varied choice of walks, but take along a proper map as well

NETWORK

▶ www.travelpod.com Reports, tips and experiences made by the travel blog community, from profound to superficial, from hardly worth mentioning to extremely savvy

▶ www.tripsay.com This is the place to filter out some good tips from the community; in English

▶ www.couchsurfing.org Individual travellers who want to get to know the locals have their choice of couches along the coast, in Valencia and elsewhere. In no way can we guarantee that you will actually be greeted the way you expected to be …

TRAVEL TIPS

ARRIVAL

✈ The international airports in the region are in Valencia, Alacant and Murcia. All three are included in the flight plans of many carriers but their timetables change frequently. There are however many connections depending on the season; Valencia is flown to by many airlines including British Airways, EasyJet and other carriers. There are also regular charter flights to Alacant and Murcia.

🚗 From the south of England, the main overland route is from Dover via Calais, Paris and Lyon to the Mediterranean and then past Perpignan and Barcelona towards the south. You will have to pay motorway tolls in France; in Spain there is a difference between the *autopistas* (motorways) that are subject to charges and the free *autovías* (main roads). You will find help on the internet from the free route planners such as *www.viamichelin. com*; they not only recommend various routes but also calculate the costs of the tolls you will have to pay on the motorways in France and Spain.

🚆 Travelling from London to the Costa Blanca is possible but takes a long time and you will need to change in Paris and Barcelona. For information on the connections between London and Barcelona, see *www.raileurope.co.uk*; information on railway travel in Spain is available under *www.renfe.com*.

🚌 Eurolines, part of the National Express service provides coaches from London to Alacant, but you have to change twice, once in Lille and once in Barcelona. You will also need a good book and a lot of patience. The advantage, however, is that the ticket is quite reasonable. For more information and price enquiries, see *www. nationalexpress.com*

RESPONSIBLE TRAVEL

It doesn't take a lot to be environmentally friendly whilst travelling. Don't just think about your carbon footprint whilst flying to and from your holiday destination but also about how you can protect nature and culture abroad. As a tourist it is especially important to respect nature, look out for local products, cycle instead of driving, save water and much more. If you would like to find out more about eco-tourism please visit: *www.ecotourism.org*

CAMPING

Campers will find good facilities on the coast. There are not only the usual places to pitch your tent or park your caravan, some sites also rent out bungalows. You should be aware that not all camping sites are open year round and that some are only in operation from Easter to October. Information in English is available from: *www.infocamping.com* and *www.campings online.com*

CAR HIRE

The standard car rental companies have offices at the international airports; you can save money if you compare prices on the internet and book before you leave home. If you book early enough, you will get a small car for 80–90 euros a week, including mileage and taxes. The companies have different minimum ages for those hiring a car, but it is normally 21. You will need to present a credit card. Spanish companies such as *Centauro (www.centauro. net)* often have good offers but some like to work with the so-called 'petrol policy' *(política de gasoline)* trick. The 'policy' is that the customer has to pay an additional sum for a full tank when he picks up the car – this can range from around 50 to as much as 100 euros depending on the model. The car can then be returned with an empty tank, but the amount charged before will be much higher than that needed to fill it up: refunds are not possible!

BUDGETING

Coffee	£0.90/$1.50 *for a small cup of coffee with milk (cortado)*
Museum	£2.40–3.20/$3.70–5 *admission*
Leather shoes	from £47–55/$74–85 *for brand footwear*
Daily set menu	from £7/$11 *in a simple restaurant*
Bus trip	£6.30–7/$10–11 *for 100km*
Ceramics	from £3.20/$5 *for a small souvenir plate*

CUSTOMS

UK citizens do not have to pay any duty on goods brought from another EU country as long as tax was included in the price and are for private consumption. The limits are: 800 cigarettes, 400 cigarillo, 200 cigars, 1kg smoking tobacco, 10L spirits, 20L liqueurs, 90L wine, 110L beer.

Travellers from non-EU countries are allowed to enter with the following tax-free amounts: 200 cigarettes or 100 cigarillos or 50 cigars or 250g smoking tobacco. 2L wine and spirits with less 22 vol % alcohol, 1L spirits with more than 22vol % alcohol content.

Travellers to the United States who are returning residents of the country do not have to pay duty on articles purchased overseas up to the value of $800, but there are limits on the amount of alcoholic beverages and tobacco products. For the regulations for international travel for U.S. residents please see *www.cbp.gov*

DRIVING IN SPAIN

Driving under the influence (a blood alcohol concentration of more than 0.5 per mille) or while using a mobile phone carry severe penalties in Spain. It is illegal for private persons to tow cars (this must be done by an authorised towing service); the car's lights and radio must be turned off when refuelling. The maximum speed in built-up areas is 50kph (30mph), on main roads 90 or 100kph (50–60 mph) – depending on the signposts – and 120kph (75mph) on motorways. There must be two warning triangles and a reflecting high-visibility vest in your car. The accident rate in Spain is unfortunately rather high; and some drivers do not seem to know what it means to keep a safe distance and show consideration for others. Pedestrians should think twice before stepping out onto a zebra crossing and assuming that cars will stop; that can be dangerous.

EMBASSIES & CONSULATES

BRITISH EMBASSY
Paseo de la Castellana 259D, 28046 Madrid | tel. +349 17 14 63 00 | ukinspain. fco.gov.uk/en

U.S. EMBASSY
Calle Serrano 75, 28006 Madrid | tel. +349 15 87 22 40 | madrid.usembassy.gov

There is also a British Consulate in Alacant *(tel. +349 65 14 95 28)* and a U.S. Consulate in Valencia *(tel. +349 63 51 69 73)*.

ELECTRICITY

220 volt, normal European two-pin plugs.

EMERGENCY SERVICES

Tel. 112: general emergencies
Tel. 091: National Police
Tel. 092: Municipal Police

HEALTH

The European Insurance Card is valid in Spain but it is not possible to select your own doctor and dental treatment is not included. The nearest Health Centre *(Centro de Salud)* is the responsible body. You will often have to wait a long time in the emergency section *(emergencias)* of a hospital and the treatment might not always meet your expectations. To be on the safe side, you should take out additional travel insurance. It is important that the doctor treating you gives you an exact bill to enable you to get a refund when you return

home; the same applies to any medicine you need. There will no doubt be several English-speaking doctors at your destination. Articles such as sport gel and heat plasters are usually cheaper than at the chemist at home and some prescription medicines are freely available.

IMMIGRATION

Citizens of the U.K. & Ireland, U.S., Canada, Australia and New Zealand need only a valid passport to enter all countries of the EU. Children below the age of 12 need a children's passport.

INFORMATION

SPANISH TOURIST OFFICES:
– *Britain: 64 North Row | London W1K 7DE | tel. +44 20 73172011*
– *Canada: 2 Bloor Street West | Suite 3402 | Toronto, ON, M4W 3E2 | tel. +14 16 96 13 131*
– *USA: 60 East 42nd Street, Suite 5300 (53rd Floor) | New York, NY 10165-0039 | tel. +12122 65 88 22*

In the U.S., there are additional offices in Chicago, Miami and Los Angeles. In Spain, the local tourist offices *(oficina de turismo)* provide information.

INTERNET
www.spain.info (official, informative site of the Spanish Tourist Authority, well organised; *www.turismodecastellon.com* (Costa del Azahar and Castelló de la Plana); *www. comunitatvalenciana.com* (Autonomous Community of Valencia); *www.costablanca. org, www.turismocostablanca.com* (Costa Blanca); *www.murciaturistica.es* (Murcia Region, Costa Cálida); *www.turisvalencia. es* (City of Valencia); *www.rusticae.es* (small, stylish hotels off the beaten track; in Spanish and English); *www.infocosta*

blanca.com (places on the Costa Blanca, real estate, weather, events); *www.turismo demurcia.es* (City of Murcia)

INTERNET & WI-FI

Wi-Fi is increasingly available as a service at airports, in hotels and other institutions; however, there is a charge for this convenience in some hotels. In addition, there are internet cafés and centres *(ciber* or *cybercafés)* in many cities and tourist destinations but their locations change frequently. Approximate prices: 30 minutes cost 1–1.50 euros; a full hour 2–3 euros. It is often possible to use an internet terminal in public libraries free of charge if you present your passport or personal ID; sometimes you will have to wait and the equipment is not always that up to date.

LANGUAGE HOLIDAYS

Language schools in towns such as Alacant and Valencia offer various Spanish courses of all levels from beginners to advanced, and they sometimes also arrange summer camps for young people. The groups are usually small and most of the teachers highly motivated; accommodation with host families can be organised if desired. Among the addresses listed by the *Instituto Cervantes (eee.cervantes.es)* are: *Proyecto Español* in Alacant *(García Morato 41 | tel. 9 65 23 06 55 | www.proyecto-es.com)* and *Costa de Valencia* in Valencia *(Blasco Ibañéz 66 | tel. 9 63 61 03 67 | www.costa devalencia.com)*.

MONEY & CREDIT CARDS

Banks are generally open Mon–Fri 9am–2pm. Credit cards such as Visa are widely accepted and cash dispensers are standard almost everywhere.

NATURISM

Topless might be the standard on many beaches, but being completely nude is not. Naturists should go to the sections of the beaches specially reserved for this purpose *(playas naturistas)*.

NEWSPAPERS

In the holiday regions, the newspaper shops cater to their international clients. You can usually get your favourite newspaper on the same day. Spaniards are keen newspaper readers although the sports section is usually the most popular; the latest editions are usually available to be read in the pubs. The serious national papers 'La Razón', 'El Mundo' and 'El País' are good sources of information.

OPENING HOURS

There are no strictly controlled opening hours in Spain. You can assume that shops are open Mon to Sat 9.30/10am–1.30/2pm and 4.30–8pm and also on Sun in the tourist areas during the high season. The Spanish enjoy shopping in large supermarkets *(hipermarcados)* on the outskirts of towns; they are open Mon–Sat 10am–10pm without a lunch break. The opening hours of the post offices vary; some have a siesta in the afternoon but all close at around midday on Sat. Government offices are usually open Mon–Fri 9am–2pm.

PERSONAL SAFETY

Police presence has increased in those areas and cities frequented by tourists in an effort to put a stop to petty crime. But that has still not completely done away with the pickpockets. Car drivers should make sure that absolutely nothing can be seen in their cars when they leave them – not

CURRENCY CONVERTER

£	€	€	£
1	1.20	1	0.85
3	3.60	3	2.55
5	6	5	4.25
13	15.60	13	11
40	48	40	34
75	90	75	64
120	144	120	100
250	300	250	210
500	600	500	425

$	€	€	$
1	0.75	1	1.30
3	2.30	3	3.90
5	3.80	5	6.50
13	10	13	17
40	30	40	50
75	55	75	97
120	90	120	155
250	185	250	325
500	370	500	650

For current exchange rates see www.xe.com

even a ballpoint pen, a map or sunglasses! However, all in all, everyday life in Spain is no more dangerous than at home.

PHONE & MOBILE PHONE

When calling abroad: punch in *00* then the country code (UK *44*, US *1*, Ireland *353*), the area code without *0* and finally the number. The country code for Spain is *0034* followed by the telephone number. In Spain, expensive service numbers often start with *902*, and you may be put on hold for a long time; Spanish mobile phone numbers start with a *'6'*. The most economical way to use the public Telefónica phone boxes is with the prepaid cards (*tarjeta telefónicas*) that are available for 5 and 10 euros from tobacconists. The telephone centres *(locutorios)* have reasonable prices. Some mobile phone users buy Spanish prepaid cards (e.g. from *Amena* or *Orange*).

PHOTOGRAPHY

Memory cards, CDs and other photographic accessories are often more expensive in Spain, while batteries are usually cheaper. Note that photography is not allowed in some churches and museums.

POST

Letters up to 20g and postcards to European countries usually only take a few days to reach their destination. Postage always increases at the beginning of the year. Stamps are available from post offices and tobacconists *(tabacos)*.

PRICES

The price increases in recent years mean that Spain is no longer a country where everything is much cheaper than at home. Some things have remained less expensive (wine, public transport, fruit, vegetables), others are now on a par or more expensive (an evening meal, for example). The fact that an additional VAT *(IVA, 8 percent)* is added to the bill at the end is often only indicated in the small print. Some water and amusement parks charge exorbitant entrance fees.

PUBLIC TRANSPORT

Buses are the most popular means of transport in the region and there is an excellent network of services. Bus prices are usually lower than those of the railway and connections are more frequent.

Each town of any size has a bus stop or central bus terminus *(estación de autobuses)*. The signposts *estación de Renfe* will guide you to the train station.

TIPPING

The Spanish are not fanatical about tipping a fixed percentage. Satisfied guests leave 5–10 percent extra in restaurants. In pubs, you can round up the bill. Taxi drivers do not expect to be tipped.

WHERE TO STAY

Accommodation ranges from the simple bed and breakfast *(pension)* or guesthouse *(hostal)* to luxury hotels. *NH (www.nh-hotels.com)* and *Tryp* or *Meliá (www.solmelia.com)*, as well as the *Paradores (www.parador.es)*, are among the best hotel chains. Country houses *(casa rurales)* are becoming increasingly trendy. However, if you decide to stay in one, make sure to note the GPS coordinates or print out a sketch of how to get there. The Rusticae chain specialises in providing such charming and exclusive accommodation *(www.rusticae.es)*. Those on a tighter budget can stay in the youth hostels *(www.reaj.com)*. Room prices in Spain do not usually include breakfast, but some hotels require that their guests book half or full board.

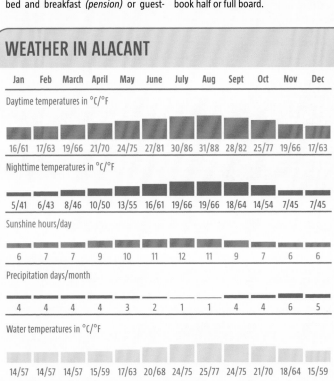

WEATHER IN ALACANT

	Jan	Feb	March	April	May	June	July	Aug	Sept	Oct	Nov	Dec
Daytime temperatures in °C/°F	16/61	17/63	19/66	21/70	24/75	27/81	30/86	31/88	28/82	25/77	19/66	17/63
Nighttime temperatures in °C/°F	5/41	6/43	8/46	10/50	13/55	16/61	19/66	19/66	18/64	14/54	7/45	7/45
Sunshine hours/day	6	7	7	9	10	11	12	11	9	7	6	6
Precipitation days/month	4	4	4	4	3	2	1	1	4	4	6	5
Water temperatures in °C/°F	14/57	14/57	14/57	15/59	17/63	20/68	24/75	25/77	24/75	21/70	18/64	15/59

USEFUL PHRASES SPANISH

PRONUNCIATION

c	before 'e' and 'i' like 'th' in 'thin'
ch	as in English
g	before 'e' and 'i' like the 'ch' in Scottish 'loch'
gue, gui	like 'get', 'give'
que, qui	the 'u' is not spoken, i.e. 'ke', 'ki'
j	always like the 'ch' in Scottish 'loch'
ll	like 'lli' in 'million'; some speak it like 'y' in 'yet'
ñ	'nj'
z	like 'th' in 'thin'

IN BRIEF

Yes/No/Maybe	sí/no/quizás
Please/Thank you	por favor/gracias
Hello!/Goodbye!/See you	¡Hola!/¡Adiós!/¡Hasta luego!
Good morning!/afternoon!/evening!/night!	¡Buenos días!/¡Buenos días!/¡Buenas tardes!/¡Buenas noches!
Excuse me, please!	¡Perdona!/¡Perdone!
May I ...?/Pardon?	¿Puedo ...?/¿Cómo dice?
My name is ...	Me llamo ...
What's your name?	¿Cómo se llama usted?/¿Cómo te llamas?
I'm from ...	Soy de ...
I would like to .../Have you got ...?	Querría .../¿Tiene usted ...?
How much is ...?	¿Cuánto cuesta ...?
I (don't) like that	Esto (no) me gusta.
good/bad/broken/doesn't work	bien/mal/roto/no funciona
too much/much/little/all/nothing	demasiado/mucho/poco/todo/nada
Help!/Attention!/Caution!	¡Socorro!/¡Atención!/¡Cuidado!
ambulance/police/fire brigade	ambulancia/policía/bomberos
May I take a photo here	¿Podría fotografiar aquí?

DATE & TIME

Monday/Tuesday/Wednesday	lunes/martes/miércoles
Thursday/Friday/Saturday	jueves/viernes/sábado
Sunday/working day/holiday	domingo/laborable/festivo
today/tomorrow/yesterday	hoy/mañana/ayer

¿Hablas español?

"Do you speak Spanish?" This guide will help you to say the basic words and phrases in Spanish.

hour/minute/second/moment	hora/minuto/segundo/momento
day/night/week/month/year	día/noche/semana/mes/año
now/immediately/before/after	ahora/enseguida/antes/después
What time is it?	¿Qué hora es?
It's three o'clock/It's half past three	Son las tres/Son las tres y media
a quarter to four/a quarter past four	cuatro menos cuarto/ cuatro y cuarto

TRAVEL

open/closed/opening times	abierto/cerrado/horario
entrance / exit	entrada/acceso salida
departure/arrival	salida/llegada
toilets/ladies/gentlemen	aseos/señoras/caballeros
free/occupied	libre/ocupado
(not) drinking water	agua (no) potable
Where is ...?/Where are ...?	¿Dónde está ...? /¿Dónde están ...?
left/right	izquierda/derecha
straight ahead/back	recto/atrás
close/far	cerca/lejos
traffic lights/corner/crossing	semáforo/esquina/cruce
bus/tram/U-underground/	autobús/tranvía/metro/
taxi/cab	taxi
bus stop/cab stand	parada/parada de taxis
parking lot/parking garage	parking/garaje
street map/map	plano de la ciudad/mapa
train station/harbour/airport	estación/puerto/aeropuerto
ferry/quay	transbordador/muelle
schedule/ticket/supplement	horario/billete/suplemento
single/return	sencillo/ida y vuelta
train/track/platform	tren/vía/andén
delay/strike	retraso/huelga
I would like to rent ...	Querría ... alquilar
a car/a bicycle/a boat	un coche/una bicicleta/un barco
petrol/gas station	gasolinera
petrol/gas / diesel	gasolina/diesel
breakdown/repair shop	avería/taller

FOOD & DRINK

Could you please book a table for tonight for four?	Resérvenos, por favor, una mesa para cuatro personas para hoy por la noche.
on the terrace/by the window	en la terraza/junto a la ventana

The menu, please/	¡El menú, por favor!
Could I please have ...?	¿Podría traerme ... por favor?
bottle/carafe/glass	botella/jarra/vaso
knife/fork/spoon	cuchillo/tenedor/cuchara
salt/pepper/sugar	sal/pimienta/azúcar
vinegar/oil/milk/cream/lemon	vinagre/aceite/leche/limón
cold/too salty/not cooked	frío/demasiado salado/sin hacer
with/without ice/sparkling	con/sin hielo/gas
vegetarian/allergy	vegetariano/vegetariana/alergía
May I have the bill, please?	Querría pagar, por favor.
bill/receipt/tip	cuenta/recibo/propina

SHOPPING

pharmacy/chemist	farmacia/droguería
baker/market	panadería/mercado
butcher/fishmonger	carnicería/pescadería
shopping centre/department store	centro comercial/grandes almacenes
shop/supermarket/kiosk	tienda/supermercado/quiosco
100 grammes/1 kilo	cien gramos/un kilo
expensive/cheap/price/more/less	caro/barato/precio/más/menos
organically grown	de cultivo ecológico

ACCOMMODATION

I have booked a room	He reservado una habitación.
Do you have any ... left?	¿Tiene todavía ...?
single room/double room	habitación individual/habitación doble
breakfast/half board/	desayuno/media pensión/
full board (American plan)	pensión completa
at the front/seafront/garden view	hacia delante/hacia el mar/hacia el jardín
shower/sit-down bath	ducha/baño
balcony/terrace	balcón/terraza
key/room card	llave/tarjeta
luggage/suitcase/bag	equipaje/maleta/bolso
swimming pool/spa/sauna	piscina/spa/sauna
soap/toilet paper/nappy (diaper)	jabón/papel higiénico/pañal
cot/high chair/nappy changing	cuna/trona/cambiar los pañales
deposit	anticipo/caución

BANKS, MONEY & CREDIT CARDS

bank/ATM/	banco/cajero automático/
pin code	número secreto
cash/credit card	en efectivo/tarjeta de crédito
bill/coin/change	billete/moneda/cambio

HEALTH

doctor/dentist/paediatrician	médico/dentista/pediatra
hospital/emergency clinic	hospital/urgencias
fever/pain/inflamed/injured	fiebre/dolor/inflamado/herido
diarrhoea/nausea/sunburn	diarrea/náusea/quemadura de sol
plaster/bandage/ointment/cream	tirita/vendaje/pomada/crema
pain reliever/tablet/suppository	calmante/comprimido/supositorio

POST, TELECOMMUNICATIONS & MEDIA

stamp/letter/postcard	sello/carta/postal
I need a landline phone card/	Necesito una tarjeta telefónica/
I'm looking for a prepaid card for my mobile	Busco una tarjeta prepago para mi móvil
Where can I find internet access?	¿Dónde encuentro un acceso a internet?
dial/connection/engaged	marcar/conexión/ocupado
socket/adapter/charger	enchufe/adaptador/cargador
computer/battery/	ordenador/batería/
rechargeable battery	batería recargable
e-mail address/at sign (@)	(dirección de) correo electrónico/arroba
internet address (URL)	dirección de internet
internet connection/wifi	conexión a internet/wifi
e-mail/file/print	archivo/imprimir

LEISURE, SPORTS & BEACH

beach/sunshade/lounger	playa/sombrilla/tumbona
low tide/high tide/current	marea baja/marea alta/corriente

NUMBERS

0	cero	14	catorce
1	un, uno, una	15	quince
2	dos	16	dieciséis
3	tres	17	diecisiete
4	cuatro	18	dieciocho
5	cinco	19	diecinueve
6	seis	20	veinte
7	siete	100	cien, ciento
8	ocho	200	doscientos, doscientas
9	nueve	1000	mil
10	diez	2000	dos mil
11	once	10 000	diez mil
12	doce	1/2	medio
13	trece	1/4	un cuarto

NOTES

FOR YOUR NEXT HOLIDAY ...

MARCO POLO TRAVEL GUIDES

- PACKED WITH INSIDER TIPS
- BEST WALKS AND TOURS
- FULL-COLOUR PULL-OUT MAP
  AND STREET ATLAS

ROAD ATLAS

The green line ▬▬▬ indicates the Trips & Tours (p. 90–95)
The blue line ▬▬▬ indicates The perfect route (p. 30–31)

All tours are also marked on the pull-out map

Photo: Beach near Alacant

Exploring Costa Blanca

The map on the back cover shows how the area has been sub-divided

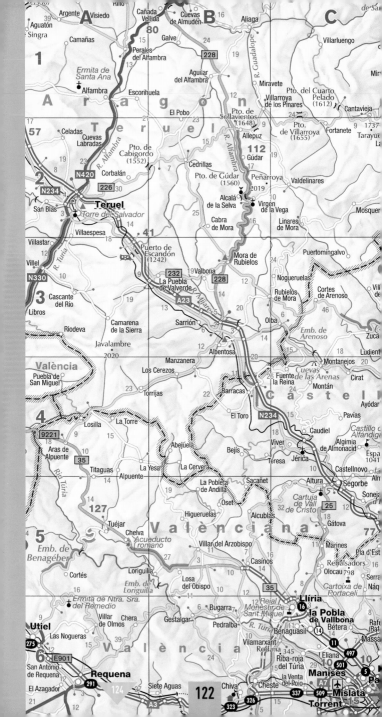

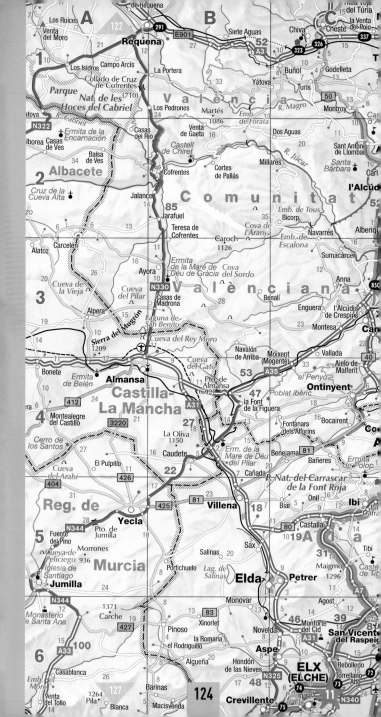

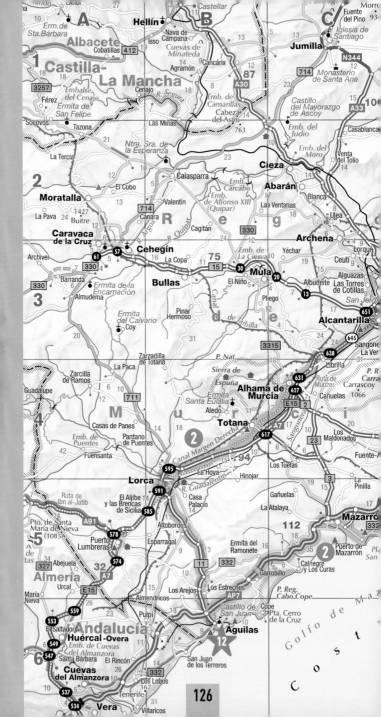

KEY TO ROAD ATLAS

18 — **26**	Motorway with junctions / Autobahn mit Anschlussstellen
=====	Motorway under construction / Autobahn in Bau
I	Toll station / Mautstelle
O	Roadside restaurant and hotel / Raststätte mit Übernachtung
⊛	Roadside restaurant / Raststätte
⊛	Filling-station / Tankstelle
═══□═══	Dual carriage-way with motorway characteristics with junction / Autobahnähnliche Schnellstraße mit Anschlussstelle
━━━━	Trunk road / Fernverkehrsstraße
━━━━	Thoroughfare / Durchgangsstraße
━━━━	Important main road / Wichtige Hauptstraße
────	Main road / Hauptstraße
-----	Secondary road / Nebenstraße
───────	Railway / Eisenbahn
🚗	Car-loading terminal / Autozug-Terminal
·−·−·−·	Mountain railway / Zahnradbahn
⊢∘∘∘∘∘∘∘⊣	Aerial cableway / Kabinenschwebebahn
···········	Railway ferry / Eisenbahnfähre
──🚘──	Car ferry / Autofähre
− − − −	Shipping route / Schifffahrtslinie
━━━━	Route with beautiful scenery / Landschaftlich besonders schöne Strecke
Alleenstr. ··········	Tourist route / Touristenstraße
XI-V	Closure in winter / Wintersperre
× × × × ×	Road closed to motor traffic / Straße für Kfz gesperrt
8% ◄	Important gradients / Bedeutende Steigungen
🚐	Not recommended for caravans / Für Wohnwagen nicht empfehlenswert
🚐	Closed for caravans / Für Wohnwagen gesperrt
☀	Important panoramic view / Besonders schöner Ausblick

* *Castell de Tibi* * *la Covatilla*	Of interest: culture - nature / Sehenswert: Kultur - Natur
∿	Bathing beach / Badestrand
▭ ▭	National park, nature park / Nationalpark, Naturpark
▒	Prohibited area / Sperrgebiet
♁	Church / Kirche
♁	Monastery / Kloster
♔	Palace, castle / Schloss, Burg
♗	Mosque / Moschee
♖ ♖ ♖ ♖	Ruins / Ruinen
⚲	Lighthouse / Leuchtturm
♙	Tower / Turm
∩	Cave / Höhle
∴	Archaeological excavation / Ausgrabungsstätte
▲	Youth hostel / Jugendherberge
⌂	Isolated hotel / Allein stehendes Hotel
⌂	Refuge / Berghütte
▲	Camping site / Campingplatz
✈	Airport / Flughafen
✈	Regional airport / Regionalflughafen
✈	Airfield / Flugplatz
─·─·─	National boundary / Staatsgrenze
─────	Administrative boundary / Verwaltungsgrenze
⊖	Check-point / Grenzkontrollstelle
⊖	Check-point with restrictions / Grenzkontrollstelle mit Beschränkung
MADRID	Capital / Hauptstadt
VALÈNCIA	Seat of the administration / Verwaltungssitz
▬	Trips & Tours / Ausflüge & Touren
▬	Perfect route / Perfekte Route
★	MARCO POLO Highlight / MARCO POLO Highlight

INDEX

This index lists all sights, museums, and destinations, plus the names of important people and key words featured in this guide. Numbers in bold indicate a main entry.

WRITE TO US

e-mail: info@marcopologuides.co.uk

Did you have a great holiday?
Is there something on your mind?
Whatever it is, let us know!
Whether you want to praise, alert us
to errors or give us a personal tip –
MARCO POLO would be pleased to
hear from you.
We do everything we can to provide the
very latest information for your trip.

Nevertheless, despite all of our authors'
thorough research, errors can creep in.
MARCO POLO does not accept any
liability for this. Please contact us by
e-mail or post.

MARCO POLO Travel Publishing Ltd
Pinewood, Chineham Business Park
Crockford Lane, Chineham
Basingstoke, Hampshire RG24 8AL
United Kingdom

PICTURE CREDITS
Cover photograph: Xàbia/Jávea, sandy La Granadella Bay (Laif: Schulz)
Steve Anderson (16 centre); A. Drouve (1 bottom); DuMont Bildarchiv: Widmann (front flap left, 2 centre top, 6, 36, 54, 66, 104/105, 106 top); Friedrichsmeier: Widmann (7); © fotolia.com: CORRADO RIVA (16 bottom), matthi (16 top); R. M. Gill (front flap right, 30 right, 39, 42, 68, 107); Huber: Gräfenhain (2 bottom, 9, 10/11, 12/13, 18/19, 44/45, 73, 75, 100/101), Schmid (2 centre bottom, 3 top, 24/25, 26 left, 32/33, 56/57, 70, 120/121), Taylor (15); Laif: Eid (85, 93), Hub (8, 52), Jonkmanns (34, 58, 106 bottom), Raach (40), Schulz (1 top); Look: Pompe (92); Mas de Canicattí SL (17 top); mauritius images: Alamy (4, 55, 62/63, 82/83, 99), imagebroker (Boenisch) (48, 65, 77, 80, 87, 94), Pixtal (26 right); OROSCO PRODUCCIONES MIRANDA SL.: Okusfokus (Gustavo Parades) (17 bottom); T. Stankiewicz (3 bottom, 60, 90/91); White Star: Gumm (2 top, 3 centre, 5, 27, 28, 29, 46, 51, 78/79, 96/97), Steinert (20); T. P. Widmann (23, 28/29, 30 left, 82 top, 89, 103, 104, 105)

1st Edition 2013
Worldwide Distribution: Marco Polo Travel Publishing Ltd, Pinewood, Chineham Business Park,
Crockford Lane, Basingstoke, Hampshire RG24 8AL, United Kingdom. Email: sales@marcopolouk.com
© MAIRDUMONT GmbH & Co. KG, Ostfildern
Chief editors: Michaela Lienemann (concept, managing editor), Marion Zorn (concept, text editor)
Author: Andreas Drouve; editor: Jochen Schürmann
Programme supervision: Anita Dahlinger, Ann-Katrin Kutzner, Nikolai Michaelis
Picture editor: Gabriele Forst
What's hot: wunder media, Munich
Cartography road atlas & pull-out map: © MAIRDUMONT, Ostfildern
Design: milchhof : atelier, Berlin; Front cover, pull-out map cover, page 1: factor product munich
Translated from German by Robert Scott McInnes; editor of the English edition: Sarah Trenker
Prepress: M. Feuerstein, Wigel
Phrase book in cooperation with Ernst Klett Sprachen GmbH, Stuttgart, Editorial by Pons Wörterbücher
All rights reserved. No part of this book may be reproduced, stored in a retrieval system or transmitted in any form or by any means (electronic, mechanical, photocopying, recording or otherwise) without prior written permission from the publisher.
Printed in Germany on non-chlorine bleached paper.

DOS & DON'TS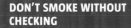

How to avoid annoying people or making a fool of yourself

DON'T SMOKE WITHOUT CHECKING

Now that Spain's politicians have taken up the cudgels against smokers, it is no longer possible to light up wherever you feel like it. Some hotels have rooms for smokers, but smoking is otherwise completely forbidden in bars, cafés and restaurants. This has led to a new meeting place: outside the main entrance.

DON'T TAKE OFF

Speed humps have become standard in many towns in an attempt to make drivers slow down. Unfortunately, not all of these 'sleeping policemen' are clearly visible, so pay attention or you may find yourself taking off.

DON'T SLIP

Spain's Mediterranean coast has a wonderful climate but that does not completely rule out rain. Some of the attractive paving on the promenades does not react well to too much water and becomes very slippery, so be careful!

DON'T PARK ILLEGALLY

In the towns, this applies to the areas with yellow (no parking) or blue lines (parking with a ticket). Flood plains, such as roads in former river beds, that are not immediately recognisable as such, can be tricky. The water often collects there when it rains; sometimes there are *zona inundable* signs to warn drivers. Police show no mercy when it comes to illegal parking. The fines *(multas)* and tow trucks *(grúa)* can put quite a dent in your holiday budget!

DON'T EXPECT THE OFF-SEASON TO BE QUIET

After the hordes of summer holidaymakers have left, many hotels use the time to renovate and improve their establishments. It can happen that the pool is closed and that there is quite a lot of building noise. Check in advance!

DON'T CONFUSE A CLUB WITH A CLUB

You could be excused for thinking that the 'clubs' you often see in Spain are the same as at home – a nightclub or place to go dancing. You would be very wrong! The red flashing light gives it away; the club is nothing more than a brothel. These establishments are usually on the outskirts of the cities and on busy roads.

DON'T SIT DOWN NEXT TO PEOPLE YOU DO NOT KNOW

If you see some free chairs at a table in a busy restaurant or café, you might feel like asking the people sitting there if they mind you joining them. But don't! Not only is this practice unknown in Spain, it would make the Spaniards feel uncomfortable, annoyed even, and could result in them getting up and leaving the restaurant.